TELLING TALES

Starting-Points for Personal and Social Education

John Goodwin *and* Bill Taylor

Edward Arnold

A division of Hodder & Stoughton

LONDON   BALTIMORE   MELBOURNE   AUCKLAND

Acknowledgements

Many people have helped in the publication of this book and the authors are indebted to them all. In particular they would like to thank the following: Art Blackburn, Caroline Caine, Alison Dimbleby, Anne Eardley, Charlotte, Linda and Sam Goodwin, Ann Jordan, Gordon Lamont, Mick Lovely, Claire Manley, Geoff Readman, Helen Stewart, Allison Sunley and Lyn Walton.

© 1988 John Goodwin and Bill Taylor

First published in Great Britain 1988

British Library Cataloguing in Publication Data

Goodwin, John, *1944–*

Telling tales; starting-points for personal and social education.
1. Great Britain, Secondary schools. Moral & social education —— For teaching
I. Title   II. Taylor, Bill, *1957–*
373'.01.'140941

ISBN 0 7131 8542 2

Typeset in Cheltenham Book by Gecko Ltd, Bicester, Oxon
Printed and bound in Great Britain for Edward Arnold, the educational, academic and medical publishing division of Hodder and Stoughton Limited, Mill Road, Dunton Green, Sevenoaks, Kent by Richard Clay Ltd, Bungay, Suffolk

Contents

Preface

Telling Tales is a collection of original stories for use as starting-points for Personal and Social Education lessons in the secondary school. The material is contemporary in content and relates to 'ordinary' people and those with whom young people can easily identify. The stories vary in style and tone. Some are comic while others are more serious. We intend the material to raise issues and questions rather than attempting to impose a particular set of values.

A short introduction to each story points up the relevant theme and after each story there are topics for discussion, suggestions for written work, role-playing, 'hot seating' and games. These active learning methods enable very real and deep issues to be explored through the safety of a fictitious context. They provide pupils with the confidence to explore and challenge attitudes and assumptions. An appendix suggests issues arising from the stories that teachers may wish to develop.

1 RELATIONSHIPS

Bernie's Family

Bernie Watts is thirteen. He doesn't think his family treats him fairly. These are the facts, as he sees them.

Nothing personal, but I've been having doubts about my family. I'm trying to think of how I can describe them without being uncharitable but it's not easy. There's my mum and my dad and my kid sister. I've known them for years. We live in the same house. We have meals together and watch telly and go on holidays once a year. And yet I can't help feeling that none of them really understands me. None of them seems to appreciate what I want.

Take Sally, my kid sister, for instance. She's ten years old and heavily into ponies and ballet dancing. We haven't got much in common. Now, Sally's problem is she's so selfish. Last Saturday there I was watching Big Daddy knocking lumps off Giant Haystacks on the box, generally minding my own business, when in waltzes Sally in her jodhpurs and riding hat. She takes one look at the telly and turns her nose up. 'You're not watching that rubbish, are you?' she says. 'There's rhythmic gymnastics on the other side.' When I quite reasonably point out that I'm enjoying the wrestling and if you dare touch that switch I'll dangle you out the window by your pigtails, she calls me a 'big baby' and goes and sulks behind the sofa. You can see what I'm up against. I don't mind being called a baby – even though actually I am three years two months four days six hours and twelve minutes older than her – but sulking! I ask you, it's nothing less than emotional blackmail. Needless to say, there we were two minutes later sitting side by side watching some girl prancing about waving coloured ribbons over her head. Sally always gets her way. I'm not sure why I let her do it, except that she has a knack of always making me feel as though I'm in the wrong. I've considered resorting to physical violence on frequent occasions but I know that it would only make me feel worse.

Then there's my mum. Now, my mum's all right in small doses. If I see her around the house I generally make a point of smiling and saying hello. She's not such a bad sort; she likes a bit of a chat now and then. She's dead good at cooking and making beds and all that sort of thing, and she never moans about my untidy bedroom more than twice in one week. I suppose on the face of it she's no worse than any other mother really. But she understands me no more than my sister. My mum has an uncanny knack of constantly showing me up in front of my mates. I'm not saying she does it deliberately, but it's becoming an alarmingly frequent occurrence. The worst instance of this happened only last Thursday. I'd invited Pincher Perkins round to stay for the night. I had a feeling it would be a regrettable thing to do from the outset, but since I'd stopped up his house twice the week before I felt morally obliged to reciprocate (as they say in dictionaries). The evening started well enough. My mum served up egg and chips for tea and not once during the meal did she mention dirty socks or lavatory seats or anything embarrassing like that. After tea Pincher and I went off conkering and before we knew, it was getting dark and time for kip. We set up the camp bed on my bedroom floor and were just tucking in to a couple of chocolate digestives when my mum comes in. She comes up to my room every night and always says the same thing. But she wouldn't say it tonight, surely? Not in front of Pincher? Surely not? But of course, she did say it. 'Hello dears,' she beamed, 'I've just come to tuck you in.' After that, Pincher Perkins couldn't sleep for laughing. Next day it was all round the third year at school that Bernie Watts' mum tucks him in at night. I was a laughing stock. Parents take a lot of forgiving sometimes.

If anything, my dad's worse. I mean, he doesn't make me look stupid but that's mainly because most of the time he doesn't even know I'm there. He's always too busy reading the paper or cleaning his pipe. Occasionally he'll say things like 'a bird in the hand is worth two in the bush' or 'never count your chickens in one basket'. Frankly I don't know what he's on about most of the time. It's impossible to have a decent, reasonable conversation with my dad. You can't say, 'Wotcher dad, how's it going?' He's no good at reasonable conversations. He can tell you how long it takes to get to Jupiter and back, or why bald-headed eagles can't fly backwards, but day-to-day stuff is quite beyond him. If you tell my dad anything at all he'll just nod his head wisely and say 'That's interesting'. I'll say, 'Hey dad, I scored a goal in football today' or 'Hey dad, I got eighty-seven per cent in my maths' and he'll nod and say 'That's interesting'. I reckon if I came home and told him I'd just freefalled from the top of the Eiffel Tower without a parachute he'd still only nod and say 'That's interesting'. I'm not entirely convinced that he ever listens to me.

Sometimes I lie in bed at nights and wonder what I've done to deserve a family like this. I mean, I know it could be worse. We don't scream and shout at each other, nobody orders me about. I get a fair amount of pocket money and at consistently regular intervals. My dad doesn't get drunk and sing rugby songs like Pincher's old man. My mum isn't thirty-eight stone and reeking of sweet perfume. My sister does have the good grace to spend most of her time riding and dancing, so I don't have to see too much of her. I know that in some ways I've a lot to be grateful for. But there's still no denying that things aren't as perfect as they ought to be. There's no denying that each member of my family has a knack of doing things that annoy me. None of them seems to think about how I feel. I'm not one to complain but honestly, is it cricket?

---

1 Discuss the following:
   (a) Are Bernie's complaints reasonable?
   (b) How do you think other members of the Watts family see Bernie?

2 Write your own account of your family, describing what you see to be their good and bad points.

3 In small groups, act out one of the following scenes:
   (a) A family dispute centred around a clash of television programmes. Who is most likely to win the argument and get their way?
   (b) A family outing that goes wrong.
   (c) Parents deciding to go away together, leaving the children to look after themselves for a few days. How do they cope? What happens and how do the parents react when they get back?

4 As a whole group, play the elimination game, 'Happy Families'.

   The group sits in a circle with one person left standing in the middle. Everyone else in the circle has a chair to sit on. Going around the circle, each person is labelled in sequence brother, sister, mum, dad or cousin.
      The person in the middle is also given a label, and must then try to sit down on one of the chairs in the circle. To do this s/he names a family member (eg. sister, dad). Anyone with that label must move to another chair and the namer attempts to sit down in one of the empty chairs while the others are changing places. The person then left standing without a chair is eliminated and the last person to sit down loses their chair and becomes the new namer.
      As the game progresses fewer and fewer chairs and players remain. The object is to try and remember each person's label, so that if you become the namer you have a chance to eliminate players by naming a label that has only one player left in the game and who is then obliged to give up his/her seat and leave the circle.
      The game continues until there are only two players left – a namer and a family label. The last namer wins or loses by his/her ability to

successfully name the label of the player in the chair.

If the namer names a label that has already been exhausted (eg. if s/he names 'aunt' when there are no aunts left), the namer is eliminated and can nominate a new namer who then gives up their chair and takes over in the middle. With a larger group, more lables can be used. If at any time the namer calls out 'Happy Families' everyone must change places.

Leaving Home

There comes a time when young people feel the need to cut the apron strings that tie them to their parents. The need for independence is a normal part of growing up.

Mary looked into the open suitcase. Inside, neatly laid out, were her three favourite summer skirts, clean underwear, night-dress, toothbrush and her writing set. It didn't look much, but the suitcase was now full so everything else would have to be left behind. She looked around the bedroom and thought about the things she would miss: the Mickey Mouse alarm clock, her prize collection of Enid Blyton picture books, Cedric the Caterpillar and Ernest Bear. She would dearly have loved to have taken the toys with her, but there was no place for such things in the big outside world where everyone walked around with stern unsmiling faces and grunted at each other. Life for Mary would never be the same again.

She closed the suitcase and locked it. From the wardrobe she took her duffle coat and put it on. It felt rather damp and cold. She knew that she didn't really need a heavy coat in the middle of August, but she'd surely be glad of it by the time winter came around. Picking up the suitcase, Mary went to the door and left her cosy little bedroom for the last time.

Mrs Thomas was in the kitchen peeling potatoes. Mary tried to reach the front door without being noticed, but Mrs Thomas had seen the girl on the stairs and, putting down her peeler, came to the kitchen door to say her goodbyes.

'You're going then?' asked Mrs Thomas, needlessly.

'Yes,' Mary replied.

'I was just going to make a brew. Do you fancy a cup before you go?'

Typical, thought Mary, trying to delay me. The girl shook her head and pulled at the suitcase that was tugging her arm with its weight.

'Very well then,' said Mrs Thomas, 'I suppose it's best to get off before it's dark. By the way, where are you going?'

Mary paused. What should she tell her? Mary's plans were rather vague but she ought to say something. 'North,' she told Mrs Thomas.

'North?'

'Yes.'

'By train?'

'Yes.'

'In that case, maybe I could give you a lift to the station, it's no trouble.'

Mary declined the offer. Again it was typical of her to be polite and co-operative at a time like this. Normally she was impatient and tetchy towards Mary. In fact, that was why Mary had decided to leave. Now she was being nice and it didn't make things any easier.

'I must be going now. Goodbye.' With that Mary turned and left the house.

Mary walked the length of Carlyle Street and halfway along Dalton Avenue before she paused for breath. The suitcase was heavier than she'd expected and the combined effect of the hot sun and the duffle coat made her feel exhausted. She sat down in a bus shelter and took off the coat, folding it neatly and placing it on top of the case. She was surprised that she felt so tired, and still confused about where she was going to go or what she was going to do. What was needed was a short rest. Mary leaned back on the bench and closed her eyes.

'Oi, you!' The harsh voice woke Mary abruptly. She opened her eyes to find a bus parked in the road beside her. She was puzzled, it hadn't been there a moment ago. The bus door was open and the driver inside was sitting drumming his fingers on the steering wheel, impatient, waiting.

'You getting on or what?'

Mary looked uncertain.

'Look kid, I ain't got all day, I'm late as it is.'

Mary got to her feet and stepped up into the bus. The automatic door hissed closed behind her and the engine, which had been purring quietly, began to growl and shudder as the bus prepared to pull away from the stop. What was she doing? She was locked inside a bus with no idea of her destination and with no money to pay for the fare. In a sudden panic she started to bang furiously on the door, begging it to swing open.

'What do you think you're up to?' the driver asked.

'You're wrong,' Mary stuttered, 'I'm not going, it's a mistake. Let me go, let me get off.'

'OK, OK,' replied the driver. The bus doors opened, and Mary climbed quickly down the steps. She heard the driver mutter a few angry words before the bus pulled away from her and disappeared into the distance. She felt confused and uncertain. Then found herself running frantically, tearing wildly across the road to the accompaniment of a vexed car horn and back along Carlyle Street. It was only when she had reached the house and pushed open the front door that she remembered her bag and coat, still lying at the bus stop in Dalton Avenue.

Mrs Thomas heard the commotion in the hall and came out of the kitchen, wiping her hands on her apron. Mary looked at her and started to cry.

'Mary, whatever's happened?' Mrs Thomas asked, picking the small girl up in her arms and comforting her.

'I want Cedric,' Mary said between sobs. 'I can't go without Cedric.'

'But I thought you said you were too old for Cedric,' Mrs Thomas replied.

Mary smiled and shook her head. Maybe she wasn't ready for the big world after all. 'Mum,' she said, 'do you mind if I come back now?'

Mrs Thomas smiled. 'And how long are you going to stay this time?'

'For ages,' Mary answered. 'Till I'm ten at least.'

1 Discuss the following:
   (a) Have you ever packed your bags and left home? If so, can you remember your reasons for going, and how long you stayed away?
   (b) Why do you think Mary's mother seemed so unconcerned about her daughter leaving?
   (c) At what age do you feel young people are ready to be independent?

2 As a group, form a semi-circle of chairs and select a volunteer to role play a character who has recently left home. The volunteer is 'hot seated' and sits in front of the group who can then ask questions about his/her experience. The idea is not to intimidate or 'catch out' the role-player but, through interview, to build up a storyline about leaving home. You may find you want to interview other characters that the role-player introduces into the discussion (e.g. friends, family etc). Once you have established the situation through 'hot seating', you could enact key scenes e.g: at home, the day before leaving; the first night away from home; meeting with parents a week or so after leaving home. Obviously the precise nature of the scenes will depend upon the information received during the 'hot seating'. Consider the details of why the person has left, and the possible consequences of the action.

Grey Hair

Do you dread the thought of old age? If you could be any age you liked, what would it be? Would you be younger or older than you are now? Perhaps not many of you would choose to be over sixty. Lyn, who is sixteen, is thinking about age.

Why can't people forget their age? Does it really matter if you're fourteen or forty? Why can't people grow old gracefully instead of trying to pretend they are younger than they really are?

Take my mother for example. She was forty last month. Talk about crisis. She wouldn't have a special party, didn't want any birthday cards, presents weren't welcome. Why? Just because she had reached the tender age of forty. When Dad sent her a cheeky card she went wild. So, it was a bit rude, but Mum just couldn't see the joke and sulked in the house all day long.

Another thing, she can't stand the thought of grey hair. A few years ago the odd grey hair started to appear amongst the brown. With devil-like cunning she would stand in front of the mirror in the bedroom and hunt for hours for the offending grey strand. Once found she would waste no time in destroying the evidence with a snip of the scissors.

But she was doomed to fail and soon the grey outnumbered the brown. If she wasn't to have a skinhead cut there was no way she could disguise the grey curse. A new plan was needed. It was called 'henna' and it arrived to save the damsel from distress. Just like the American Cavalry it was swift, sure to succeed and deadly to the enemy. In case you don't already know, henna is a natural dye made from a tropical shrub and its shoots and leaves dye your hair (or anything else for that matter) a deep reddish-brown colour. Mum didn't use a tropical plant in the bathroom, just a brown plastic bottle with a sticker marked 85p on it. But once again it was kept a secret from the rest of the family and the offending bottle discreetly hidden behind the toilet pan. Ridiculous isn't it? Why go to all that fuss? I know I wouldn't do it. But Mum kept that bottle and replacement bottles hidden there for months. Only thing was it wasn't a secret, the whole family knew, but Mum was so touchy about it we didn't dare mention it. So the secret obliteration of the grey hairs continued unabated. Until disaster struck!.

Mum went to buy the henna as usual but the shop had sold out. Being in a hurry, and not wishing to have any tell-tale roots showing, she bought a trial offer of an alternative dye. Waiting until the house was empty, she applied the new trial offer to her hair. 'Let the shampoo remain on the scalp for fifteen minutes,' it said on the bottle. Mum settled down to read Mills and Boon little knowing the havoc that was being wreaked. Time to rinse the scalp. What's this? A strange colour? Just a minute – my hair is purple! Panic. Rinse again. No difference – my hair has gone a weird colour! More panic, more water, but purple is here to stay.

One hour later I returned from the disco. Mum had a towel round her head and was in tears. I said to myself: This isn't right. I'm the teenager, I'm the one who's supposed to be going through an identity crisis. Then Mum takes the towel off and I think – Mum wants to be a punk – strange but what's wrong with that? After all, purple hair is rather trendy.

Joking apart, something happened that night. Mum put her head on my shoulder and cried her eyes out. Never known anything like it before. I tried to comfort her and at last I succeeded. We've not sat and talked like that for years. As I'd grown older we'd grown apart. She told me the whole story and I agreed to go with her to the chemist the following day. We saw the chemist and he gave us something to remove the purple colour but warned Mum that her hair must remain its natural colour – no henna or any other dye until it had all grown out. If not, her hair was likely to fall out.

All that was some time ago and in a strange kind of way it worked out for the best. Mum and I are now much closer. Everyone says how much grey hair suits her, as indeed it does. And finally there is no pretence; Mum can age gracefully. Let's hope when I get to forty that I won't be afraid of grey hair.

1 This story explores a mother/daughter relationship. Discuss whether you think your parents sometimes behave unreasonably. Are there times when you behave unreasonably to your parents? Have there been times when you have caused your parents real worry? In the story Lyn says, 'Mum and I are now much closer.' Why do you think this has happened?

2 Collect a couple of photographs taken when you were much younger. Carefully pencil your name on the back of the photographs making sure nobody sees them. Then lay the photographs face upwards on a large table, and try to guess who the photographs depict.

A Dog's Life

Dogs are the most popular of all domestic pets, outnumbering even cats. When we talk about a 'dog's life' do we really understand what it means? I wonder if a dog could tell us?

They call me Jack. Jack Russell. I suppose I shouldn't complain. Most of my chums are called Fido, Lucky, Bonzo, Rover or Ben. I'm luckier than most but, all things considered, 'Jack Russell' is a stupid sort of name to give a Golden Retriever.

My master Cyril gave me the name. He goes around in baggy jumpers and corduroy trousers and thinks he's got a sense of humour. You've probably met loads of people like Cyril. They drag you all over the floor, or get you to sit up on your hind legs for a measly chocolate drop, or hurl whacking great sticks into the middle of ponds and expect you to go in after them. Most of the time I play along with him. It saves a lot of tears and trouble. I remember one occasion in the woods very vividly. After half an hour of chasing after a twig I decided I'd had more than enough. I mean, where's the profit in fetching something if your master is instantly going to throw it away again? But when I lay down on the ground for a rest, Cyril got quite unnecessarily het up. 'Come on Jack,' he demanded, 'you're supposed to be a retriever – retrieve!' I ignored him and went off in search of rabbits. Cyril was not best pleased. He sulked all the way home.

Mind you, Deirdre's the one I don't get on with. Deirdre does not like me and that's a fact. She's forever pushing me out of my favourite armchair, or locking me out of the dining room just as the grub is being served up, or sending me off into the garden late at night to 'do my business'. I've got no business to do at half past eleven on a bitter wintry night thank you very much.

But the person who really gets my goat is Roxanne. Roxanne is only seven years old and at the moment her chances of reaching eight without getting her fingers bitten off are slender in the extreme. Roxanne's greatest delight is poking her fingers into my ears and watching them twitch. This apparently amuses her. She is also partial to prising my mouth open and counting my teeth. She does have her good points I suppose. When she's eating sweets, I only have to adopt that silly sad expression that humans so love and she happily gives me jelly babies and toffee. However, it's small compensation for the pawing and mauling I have to suffer.

These people are only happy as long as you do what they want. All interesting activities – like digging holes in the garden, or filching freshly baked cakes from the window-sill, or scaring the living daylights out of visitors by barking and jumping up as soon as they come through the door – are out as far as humans are concerned. Sit quietly, lick a few hands and try not to exude unpleasant smells and they're happy. Try to enjoy yourself and you're in the proverbial dog-house.

They've even got me on a chain in the garden now. OK, it's quite a long chain, it allows me to roam around fairly freely, but that doesn't take away from the fact that I am a virtual prisoner in my own domain. This latest indignity came about because they thought I was trying to break down the garden fence. Actually I was doing nothing of the sort. All I was trying to do was get over into next door's backyard to see Trixie, a delightful little French poodle that I've had my eye on ever since she moved in a couple of months ago. She's a real bow-wower and by the way she barks and rushes around whenever I'm in sight I think she rather fancies me. But there's not much chance of a meaningful relationship while I'm tied to a post is there?

As the saying goes, it's a dog's life. In fact, since all I ever seem to do is lie in front of the fire, chase things and eat bowls of Winalot, it's hard to understand why they keep me here at all. I mean, really, what is the point of it all? Your guess is as good as mine.

---

1 Centre a group debate around the following statement: 'Dogs are loyal and easily trained because they're too stupid to know any better.' Use your experiences and knowledge of pet dogs to speak for or against the statement and then take a vote.

2 Discuss the following:
(a) What is the purpose of keeping pets?
(b) Why do you feel that some people care more for their pets than they do for other people?
(c) Stray dogs can be found in most towns and cities and the RSPCA kennels are constantly overcrowded. What do you feel could or should be done to solve this problem?

3 Act out one of the following scenes:
(a) A family being visited by a farmer who claims that their dog has been worrying his sheep. The farmer may at this point have already shot the dog (as he would be legally entitled to do if the dog was attacking his livestock). Where do your sympathies lie in this situation?
(b) Two dogs meeting in a park and discussing their owners. For the purpose of this scene, let's assume they're talking dogs!
(c) A child trying to persuade his/her parents to buy a dog. The parents present arguments against a pet. Can the child persuade them to change their minds?

Mini

The cars that people have can tell us something about them. Sometimes people treat their cars as if they were human beings. What does Norman's attitude to his car tell us about him?

I suppose she's not much to look at but I like her.

She's short and squat, red all over, gets hot easily. I will say this for her though, considering her age she still holds well, she's reliable and on the quiet she's a bit of a goer and all. I say on the quiet but actually she makes a lot of noise for her size, but one learns to make allowances doesn't one? It's also true to say that she's not as young as she used to be although, all things being equal, I'd not be without her.

I'm not saying we haven't had our little problems. Only last week I had to have her looked at. She'd started leaving puddles everywhere and I was getting some funny looks from folk when they passed us in the street. So I said to her, I said, 'You're having a check up old girl.' She didn't grumble too much. Credit where credit's due, she's not one to moan and rattle and make a big drama out of life's little ailments. Not that there was anything seriously wrong, mind. I always do my best to treat her properly. Once Mr Franklin got hold of her he soon put a stop to those little leaks. Now I can take her out in public with no fear of embarrassment.

My next-door neighbour, Roderick, asked me last Sunday: 'Here, Norman, why do you call it "she"?'

I naturally pretended to ignore him.

'I mean to say,' he persisted, getting rather indignant, 'it's not a "she" is it? It's only a car.'

'It may well be only a car to you,' I retorted, proving that I can be equally as shirty when the need arises, 'but Mini and I go way back. We've been together,' I told him, pointing at the glorified sardine can that passes for his sports car, 'we've been together long before that little floosie of yours was even invented.'

Roderick had no answer to that one. He huffed under his breath and went off to sulk in his greenhouse. Good riddance, if you ask me. He's a bit of a know-all is our Roderick.

I am not an unreasonable man, but there's some folk who do not appreciate the special relationship that exists between a man and his motorcar. Mini's been with me for thirteen years, we've seen a lot of life together – good times and bad times, laughter and tears – and we've learnt to understand each other. More than anything else, cars need to know who's boss. I'll give you a for instance. A couple of Sundays ago there we were merrily chugging up a none-too-stressful one in five when Mini starts to splutter and whine. Classic case of fishing for sympathy.

'Oh no you jolly well don't,' I said to her sternly. 'We'll have none of that, thank you very much.' And I decided to put my foot down on the clutch pedal and change into a lower gear. After that Mini started to behave herself and we carried on as though nothing had happened. We understand each other, you see. No names, no pack-drill, but there are some cars that'll break down soon as look at you; flashy little runners that guzzle petrol like there's no tomorrow and come to a grinding halt any time the fancy takes them. But my Mini knows her place. It's all to do with firmness. Cars need to know who's turning the ignition, so to speak, they need to realise that you are not going to be a prey to their flighty whims.

Mini knows where she stands and has proved herself to be a dependable old girl. She's well looked after. I give her a nice wash and wax every alternative Sunday, I keep an eye on the oil and water, every Friday I take her down to Mr Franklin for a couple of gallons of three star, and I am especially careful who I allow to go prodding about under her bonnet. It wouldn't do to have any old Tom, Dick or Harold fiddling around with her engine because, as we all know, cars are temperamental creatures. I think I can say with pride that I treat Mini with the respect and affection that befits her. You can keep your quadraphonics and your rear-screen wipers and your fur-lined seat covers. I believe in treating cars the simple, old-fashioned way. She does well by it. She's never happier than when she's pottering down a nice little lane at a steady thirty-five.

I have heard folk say that cars need a bit of freedom. 'Take her on to the motorway,' Roderick once suggested. 'Let her have some throttle and give her a chance to take off.' When I inquired how either of us might benefit from such a wanton display of reckless indulgence, Roderick replied, 'You want to give your mini a bit of excitement, not just leave her stuck in your poky garage getting bored.'

Of course, what Roderick and his kind fail to appreciate is that cars don't really want too much freedom. More than that, they haven't the self-control to cope with freedom. Am I supposed to step hard on the gas and let Mini crash herself into the nearest streetlamp? I should cocoa. Someone has to exercise restraint or else where would we all be? No, my Mini is much better off if I don't let her stray too far from home. She enjoys the occasional Sunday afternoon drive but, as I say, I wouldn't let a car of mine over exert herself and end up breaking down all over the place.

I know what's best for my Mini. And she knows I know. And that's the way it should be.

1 Discuss the following:
   (a) Would you say that Norman's attitude to his car is normal?
   (b) Why do you think Norman insists on referring to his mini as 'she'?
   (c) Does Norman's attitude to his car tell us anything about his attitude to people? How do you think he treats women?

2 In small groups or as a whole class attempt to 'hot seat' Norman to find out more about him. You can do this with one person taking the role of Norman whilst other members of the group ask questions about his life: e.g. Do you always call your car 'she'? Do you think men are superior to women? What did you mean when you said 'I know what's best for my Mini'?

The Empty House

In many towns and cities you will find whole streets of empty, derelict houses. The last owners have long since moved out and the places now lie disused and decaying. But these condemned buildings are still of use to some people: those who have nowhere else to live, or those who – like the brother and sister in this story – need somewhere to hide.

Brian stared at the room. In one corner there was a pile of old newspapers and cardboard. The little furniture there was broken and decrepit. But worst of all was the smell, a thick sickly stench of decay. Brian didn't like it.

'We're never stopping here, are we?'

'If you don't like it Brian you can always go back,' his sister said sharply.

'Ain't going back there.'

'Stop complaining then.'

Brian sat down on one of the suitcases and sighed loudly, deliberately. When his sister had suggested that they go away he'd imagined going back to the old house. But the old house had been sold, so Ruth had told him, and most of their parents' belongings had been stored away or auctioned. 'Don't worry,' she'd said, 'I know somewhere we can go. No one will find us.' As Brian looked at the desolate room he wondered if going away was such a good idea after all. He wondered if maybe they should have stayed at Tom and Claire's.

Ruth felt pleased with the way things were working out. She had been planning the move for weeks, ever since the day Tom had asked them to call him 'Dad'. She hadn't been happy staying with their foster parents and that was the final straw. It had been barely nine months since the accident, how could she be expected to call anyone 'Dad'? Tom and Claire tried to do things properly, she knew that, but she was equally determined that no one was going to take the place of her real parents. It had become increasingly obvious to her that she and Brian needed to get away. Somewhere private and remote, where no one could bother them, where they could be together with what they'd got left – themselves.

Wilbur Street had been empty for years. The tenants had been moved into new flats long ago, but then for some reason the council had never got round to demolishing the old houses. The house they were in was in better shape than most of the others – at least it still had floorboards and a working water tap in the backyard. All in all, it wasn't a bad place. They could be happy here.

The first few days weren't so bad. Brian even helped with some of the cleaning and one morning he went out early and came back with a newspaper and two pints of milk. Ruth thought it wise not to inquire too closely how he came by them. At least he's showing a bit of co-operation, she thought. At least he's stopped complaining about everything.

Once cleaned, the place was really quite homely. Unfortunately they could do little about the stale smell. They'd thought of unboarding the window but with no means of heating they decided against it. Better smelly than cold.

'There we are. Just like home,' Ruth said proudly.

'It'll do I suppose,' Brian replied. He couldn't help feeling there was something missing. Not just a television, or nice cushions. Even after all that work, even when they were both sitting there together, the place felt strange and empty. 'What do we do now?' he asked.

'We don't have to do anything. It's perfect.' Ruth was very pleased with herself. He hadn't seen her so happy for months. But all the same, someone had to be realistic about this.

'I mean, what're we going to do now we're here?'

'We've got books,' Ruth said, pointing to a row of mildewed paperbacks lined neatly along the wall, 'that'll keep us occupied.'

'Don't like books.'

'And there's the radio. You like listening to the radio.'

'Can't just listen to the radio all day.'

'You're not stupid Brian, you'll think of something to do.'

Ruth picked out an old book to read: *The Dream of a Princess*. Yes, she liked the sound of that. She settled herself down on the sofa. She became so engrossed in the romance that she didn't notice Brian leaving.

It was a bright, crisp day outside. The sun was dazzling after the dullness of the old room. Everything was the same – women dragging children in and out of shops, old men standing at street corners picking tobacco off their lips, kids playing street games. Nothing had changed. It was always like that. Whatever happens to you, it never changes anything. He remembered the day he'd heard about the accident. The world didn't stop, people didn't rush up to him in the street and tell him how sorry they were. And now, who cared about him and his sister? Who was bothered about what they'd done or why they'd done it?

At the bottom of Yeoman Road he stopped. He could see Tom's blue escort parked outside number seventeen. It was only five fifteen; Tom must have got back from work early. He walked slowly past the house, glancing at the white lace windows behind which Tom and Claire lived out their lives. 'I'm not going back there. No way,' Brian said under his breath, and he moved away from the house.

It was getting dark by the time he got back to Wilbur Street. Up ahead, in the shadows, he saw a figure coming towards him. It was tall, lank, dark.

'Evening,' the man said as he reached Brian.

'How do,' Brian grunted.

The man looked down at the young boy. He couldn't be more than twelve or thirteen, rather scruffy as well, 'Where do you live sonny?' he asked.

Brian smiled, 'I'll show you if you like.'

'Yes, you do that.'

'Follow me then.'

Brian went to the house at the top of Wilbur Street where he and Ruth had set up home. The man paused, muttered a few sentences into his walkie talkie, and then followed the boy into the derelict old building.

Inside, Ruth had just turned the last page of her story as Brian entered.

'Look Ruth,' he said eagerly, 'I found someone.'

---

1 Discuss the following:
(a) Do you feel it is realistic of Ruth and Brian to want to look after themselves?
(b) Is running away the best solution to their problems?
(c) What impressions do you get of Tom and Claire, the foster parents? Do you feel Ruth and Brian should go back to them?

2 Try improvising one of the following scenes:
   (a) The day Ruth and Brian receive news of their parents' accident.
   (b) Meal time at Tom and Claire's, on the night that Tom asks the
   children to call him 'Dad'.
   (c) Ruth and Brian in the derelict house. It is late at night when they
   hear the front door opening and a stranger enters. Consider who the
   stranger might be, and the possible consequences for Ruth and
   Brian.

3 Write the rest of the story, explaining what happens to Ruth and
   Brian after the policeman has found them. Think about why Brian
   invited him into the hideaway in the first place.

4 In a small group, plan and record a radio play entitled *The Derelict
   House*: some friends explore an empty house, but terrifying things
   start to happen when they open a door marked 'Strictly Private'.
   Think about how you will create the sound effects for your play.
   Remember that a radio play relies heavily on the listener's
   imagination; you are not limited by props or costume, so literally
   anything could be acted out. How imaginative and bizarre can you
   make your story?

Owning Up

*We all need friends. Perhaps you can remember the times when
friends have helped you when you had problems, or when you
were let down by people whom you believed were your friends.
Kathleen betrays her friend in 'Owning Up'. Why does this
happen?*

Kathleen sat outside the headteacher's office feeling confused and
shocked. She thought back over the events of that morning with a
mixture of disbelief and regret. Her reputation in the school had been
unblemished until that moment. She sighed, close to tears. If only she
could turn back the clock and put things right.

    Kathleen had been waiting in the corridor for twenty minutes by the
time Mrs Jackett called her into the office. Kathleen felt that strange
sensation of panic mixed with relief – the awful knowledge that
something unpleasant was about to happen but that it would soon be

over. Mrs Jackett was sitting at her desk, the light behind her, most of her face in shadow. Standing to one side of the desk was Mr Archer, the school caretaker. Kathleen remembered how often they'd exchanged smiles and jokes together. He was an elderly, jolly man, always ready with a whimsical remark or a piece of mischievous gossip about one of the teachers. But today he wasn't smiling, he didn't look friendly and harmless, he looked angry and aggrieved.

'Is this the girl?' Mrs Jackett asked the caretaker.

'That's her,' he replied curtly.

Mrs Jackett put on a pair of heavy-rimmed glasses and picked up a sheet of paper. Kathleen could just make out the writing on the paper, scribbled hurriedly in red ink.

'Now, Kathleen,' Mrs Jackett said, in a surprisingly calm voice, 'this is an extremely serious charge. What have you to say for yourself?'

Kathleen did not reply. What could she say, except that she was guilty? It was something she could scarcely bring herself to confess.

'Silence is not going to help us,' the headteacher said.

'No, Miss,' Kathleen replied.

'I'm determined to know the truth about this matter, Kathleen.' Mrs Jackett paused, put down the paper and leaned forward across the desk. When she spoke it was in a quiet, conspiratorial manner. 'Now look here, Kathleen, we know each other don't we? Your record of achievement at this school is excellent, you're well liked by both staff and fellow pupils and you've been put forward by Mr Hamlyn as a possible prefect for next term. To be honest, I find it incredible that a girl of your standing would be so foolish as to play a prank like this.'

'It was her Mrs Jackett,' the caretaker said officiously. 'I was only round the corner when I heard the glass smash. She was the only one near the window.'

'But is it not possible, Mr Archer, that someone else is responsible for the broken window? Couldn't someone have been hiding in the shed or behind the dustbins? There are plenty of hiding places in that part of the school.'

'Well, yes,' Mr Archer said, 'but she was there, Miss. I saw her. She was standing right there, broad as day.'

'I have a little theory.' The headteacher now addressed Kathleen. 'I believe that you were a witness to this incident, and that for reasons best known to yourself you are harbouring another's guilt. Let's be honest, Kathleen, girls like you do not do things like this, do they?'

Kathleen stared at the ground, thinking furiously. What was she to do now? She had done it. Mrs Jackett's judgement of character had been proved fallible. And yet, why own up to something that you never intended to do in the first place? After all, maybe it wasn't entirely her fault. She remembered Melissa's taunts: creepy Kathleen, goody two-shoes, little miss perfect! She'd always thought of Melissa as a friend. One of her best friends. But Melissa had goaded her, made her look stupid in front of the others. Melissa had driven her to smash the window, to prove that she wasn't just a teacher's stooge. Surely Melissa was just as much to blame.

'Nobody wants to be thought of as betraying a friend,' she could hear the headteacher saying, 'but I have to warn you that unless you own up and tell me who really was responsible for this escapade, I shall have no alternative but to assume that you are the only guilty party. I need not tell you what kind of effect that would have on your future career with us.'

'I don't want to get anyone into trouble,' Kathleen said.

'I appreciate that, my dear, but people should not be protected. We should all have the courage to face the consequences of our actions. Only a fool would allow herself to be made the scapegoat.'

If only Mrs Jackett understood the irony of her words. Kathleen looked at the headteacher – smiling benignly at her, and then across at the caretaker. He was looking at her severely, as though harbouring an impotent sense of misgiving. He knows, she thought; Mrs Jackett only believes what she wants to, but Mr Archer knows the truth.

'Take this, Kathleen.' Mrs Jackett handed the girl a sheet of writing paper. 'I want you to write the name of the girl who committed this act on that piece of paper. As a witness to the incident, it is your duty to help us.'

Unswayed by her sense of guilt and shame, Kathleen took the sheet of paper from Mrs Jackett's hand and rested it on the desk top. She could sense Mr Archer's disapproval as she wrote.

When Kathleen left the school some years later, she was regarded as a model pupil, with a place at university and highly regarded by the teaching staff of the school. But for Kathleen her success was still qualified by a sense of distaste as she remembered the guilty act that had saved her reputation.

---

1 Discuss what you would have done if you had been Kathleen. Should Mrs Jackett have behaved differently?

2 Make a personal timetable of how you spend your week – at home, school etc. Look at your timetable and consider the range of people you come into contact with. Are there different groups of friends represented in the list? Or do you just mix with one group of friends?

3 Decide with the help of the teacher a class list of a range of activities, for example, chewing gum, hugging Grandma, swearing etc. Then talk about who you would and wouldn't do each activity in front of. For example, would you hug Grandma in front of your mates? Then discuss the reasons for your decisions.

4 Act out one of the following scenes:
 (a) The events leading up to Kathleen breaking the window.
 (b) The named girl confronting Kathleen.
 (c) The caretaker with Kathleen immediately after the meeting with
 Mrs Jackett.

Enough is Enough

Do you judge people by first impressions? If so, you may have found that the decisions you made about some people have needed some modification after you got to know them. For Steven, this certainly proved to be the case.

None of us had ever met Mrs Crow but we all felt we knew her. She lived in a large house a mile or so outside the village. She had acres of garden that were left untended and wild. It was said that her only companions were dogs, hundreds of them by all reports, and her entourage of stray cats, undomesticated and half-tamed. It was also said that she dressed in working-men's clothes and smoked cheroots. Once we found an empty bottle of scotch whisky in her garden. No doubt there was other incriminating evidence littering the place but we rarely ventured further than the outer grounds of her garden. Rumour was that a small child once dared to go into the house and was never seen again. There were dozens of stories about the forbidden old woman: she practised witchcraft, she ate live animals, she put curses on young girls and made their hair fall out. We did not know if these stories were true, but we all hoped they might be.
 The letter arrived in a buff envelope. The handwriting on the envelope was shaky and my name was spelt incorrectly, with a 'ph' instead of a 'v'. I was twelve years old and this was the first time I'd been sent such a mysterious letter. I opened the envelope slowly, trying to contain my excitement. Inside was an old, brownish piece of paper, folded twice. It had the dead smell of dank air, or perhaps stale tobacco. I unfolded the paper and rested it on my knees. It read:
 My dear boy,
 Enough is enough. We must meet. You are invited to tea this
 Saturday. Four o'clock.
 With regards, Alice Crow.
 I reread the letter several times. I could not understand how she had known who I was or why for that matter she had chosen to write to me.

What did she mean by 'enough is enough'? There was, I felt, something strange and dangerous about this letter. I knew I should not go to the forbidden house and yet that I would do so willingly. I had been picked. Alice Crow did not know me but she had special qualities and for some dark reason she wanted to meet me. I didn't feel threatened or scared, I felt privileged.

Saturday came. I arrived at the large mysterious house, hidden away in its overgrown garden, and knocked firmly at the front door. There was no reply. I knocked again. This time I could hear a voice from the other side of the door, an old, high-pitched voice cracking and squeaking demonically: 'Go round, boy. The back door.' I thought for a moment of running home but though it seemed a wise thing to do at the time, I knew I would regret not meeting this weird lady. I had to see her. I made my way round to the back of the house.

The back door was open but I could not see the room inside. It was hard to focus against the brilliant sunlight.

'Come in, dear boy,' the voice croaked. I stepped forward into the darkness. As my eyes adjusted to the gloom I could make out a large table in the middle of the room with tea things carefully arranged at one end. The room itself looked empty at first, but then I saw her. She was standing by the open fire. She was small, stout, wearing old faded clothes. Her skin was coarse and spotted with brown marks, her hair was white and thin. The features of her face were harsh and when she smiled her thin lips parted to reveal gums and a few broken brown teeth. She laughed in a high crackle. I stared at her, unable to move. I had never seen evil before. She dug her fists into the waistband of her skirt and, shuffling from one foot to the other, beckoned me in and pointed to a wooden chair.

I took a step forward and smiled awkwardly. I could feel her piercing, glassy eyes as she stared at me wordlessly. At last she spoke again. One word, short, sharp, insistent. 'Tea?' She lifted a silver teapot and shuffled towards the table, sliding clumsily from one foot to the other. Her fingers were twisted and stiff and her hand shook as she lifted the pot. I was surprised that she managed to fill the cups with tea without spilling any. She offered me a cup-cake and then, with a loud sigh of relief, flopped into the cushioned chair beside me.

'Never grow old, dear boy,' she said, 'it's scarcely worth the effort.'

'I'll try to remember that,' I said.

'I used to run this place single-handed, my dear. Oh yes, not a speck of dust. And the garden. Pristine, dear boy. You wouldn't think it, I daresay. But nowadays, you can't conceive what it's like. It's damned annoying I can tell you. Damned annoying.'

The more she spoke, the less threatened I felt. She was beginning to seem just a lonely old lady, not a witch at all. I thought of the tales we used to tell about the mysterious Mrs Crow; she seemed so horribly ordinary by comparison.

'Well, dear boy, I suppose you're wondering why I invited you here?

Fact is, you come highly recommended.'

I was surprised to hear this.

'Miss McAllister herself recommended you. Miss McAllister is an old friend of mine. Between you and me, dear, she's a bit of an old fusspot. Never become a teacher, you'll turn into a fusspot.' She winked mischievously. 'Any road, she's got it into her head that I need some help around the place. She came to see me recently and do you know what she said? She said, "Alice, enough is enough! Help is needed urgently." Nothing much mind, someone to chop a few logs and to see to the vegetable garden. I know it's a frightful imposition, dear boy, don't imagine for a minute that you are obliged in any way, but I would appreciate a reliable young man to help out.'

So that was it! Psychic intuition had not been responsible for my invitation that Saturday afternoon but merely the recommendations of my old primary school teacher. I found myself laughing out loud. Mrs Crow smiled at me, then she too was laughing. From that moment onwards we became the best of friends.

---

1 Discuss the following:

(a) How do you think the rumours about Mrs Crow began? What was it that made children imagine she was evil?

(b) What do you think Steven will tell his friends about his visit?

2 With a partner, take turns in describing the first impressions you had of each other and compare these with your current perceptions. The partner need not necessarily be a close friend. You could also compare these impressions with how you see yourselves.

3 Choose one person from the group who is to be the subject of a rumour. As a whole group discuss a situation you will all role play, e.g. in a school classroom, at work on a building site. (The situation needs to be one where everyone knows each other.) The 'subject' is then asked to leave the room while the rest of the group make up a rumour about him/her. When the 'subject' returns, he/she has to try to discover what the rumour is by the way the group behaves and reacts. The group should try not to state too obviously the nature of the rumour but rather imply how it has affected attitudes towards the 'subject'.

When the 'subject' has discovered what the rumour is, consider what action might be taken to counteract it. Is there anything the 'subject' can do to prove the story false? Why has the rumour spread? From here it may be possible to develop other scenes to explore how, why and for what purpose rumours are spread.

First Meeting

Did your parents ever tell you how they first met? Or isn't it something you talk about? Can you imagine your mum and dad as two love-struck teenagers? Have you seen old photographs of them at a time before you were born? Some couples meet at discos, dances or at college. Others have been close friends since school days or have met at work. The following is told by Julie.

Only yesterday my parents told me how they first met and you wouldn't believe how romantic it is. When you listen to the story you'd bet it was made up but it's the truth, really it is.

It was back in 1970. My dad had gone on a camping holiday with his brother to Greece. The place was called Ios. Doesn't it sound romantic? You never saw the sea bluer, or such beautiful sea creatures says Dad. He was a student at the time and his brother was out of work. They'd not been on holiday together before and it all felt a bit strange. Both tried hard to make it work and the long journey through Europe brought them closer together. They had thumbed lifts, as they had very little money. At last they found this campsite. It was quite large, complete with shops and a bar, but very quiet for the time of year.

It happened on the second day. My mother is Dutch and they both say that it was love at first sight. She was playing a game of skittles and Dad soon found a way of joining the game. It was her long blonde hair that did it says Dad. Mum says that he was so kind and considerate. She spoke perfect English even in those days and so conversation was easy. Helena, that's my Mum's name, had a friend called Alexandra and the four of them, including my Dad's brother, Frank, spent the next two days together.

The trouble was that Alexandra and Frank didn't get on too well. Soon Frank was pestering to move on to a new campsite. Alexandra wasn't happy either. She felt her friendship with Helena was being threatened. But Mum and Dad were in love.

After some bitter arguments and tears a bargain was struck. It was agreed Mum and Dad would spend the next day alone together, but after that the two men would move on and the foursome would be finished. Dad and Mum won't say much about that day they spent together, apart from the fact that it was like being in heaven.

But a contract had been struck and the following day it was time for the men to move on. Can you imagine Mum sitting in her tent, awake at 7.30 in the morning, hearing sounds of her lover packing away his tent? They had said their goodbyes and she knew that she could not even peep out of her tent or she would run to him and break the bargain.

Frank at least was happy; it was just like old times, brother and brother. On the brothers trudged to the next campsite six miles away. Even that early in the morning the heat was unbearable. At last they arrived at the campsite and were soon settled in. Dad and Frank started snorkling and the activity brought them back together. Frank was not a strong swimmer but loved floundering about for hours looking at the sea-bed. But Dad could not forget Helena and the next day he set off back to the old campsite. He had no tent, nothing, only the thought of Helena to guide him. And there was the guilt. He had not had the courage to face Frank, but had left him a note and sneaked away. Would she still be there? Would he ever see her again? Did she care as deeply as he did or was it just another holiday romance, a three-day wonder?

The thought of their meeting back at that campsite even brings tears to my eyes.

'Hello. I've come back.'

She just looked at him and kissed him.

A year later, after exchanged letters, phone calls and visits, they were married, and I was conceived soon after.

All that was some time ago now. They don't hold hands as they walk down the road or kiss in public. But I still think they love each other. Only the love has changed, not died but developed.

---

1 Discuss the following:

(a) Do you believe in love at first sight?

(b) What qualities are needed for a lasting relationship between two people?

(c) If you had the choice would you get married?

(d) The story finishes with the words 'Only the love has changed, not died but developed'. What do you understand this to mean? In what ways might it have changed and developed?

2 Search through magazines, books and videos. What picture do they give you of love? How many different types of love do they show? Do they tell the truth about love? Look at advertisements in magazines, do they show a distorted picture of love?

Happy Ending

Many stories about lonely old people seem to end on a depressing note. However, it doesn't always have to be like that.

The ambulance drew up outside the house. Its distinct white colour shone in the gloom. A few minutes later the frail form of the old lady was carried out on a stretcher. The neighbours peeped from behind their curtains, and with knowing looks they thought: 'That's the last time we shall see her.' They waited for the inevitable to happen: a 'For Sale' notice to be put up outside the house, as a sign that one life had finished its brief span on earth.

After all, it had been bound to happen. Her husband had died the previous year after fifty years of married life. How could anyone be expected to continue living in those circumstances? There were the increasing visits by the doctor, the provision of meals on wheels and the fact that she was never seen outside the house any more. She used to go to the local shop when her husband was alive, but that had stopped months ago. Worn out by living so long, it seemed that now she only wanted to die.

But they had not taken into account the toughness of Emily Johnson and one small musical instrument.

At first Emily did not take kindly to the geriatric unit in the hospital and she fretted for the ambulance to take her back home, so she could be on her own again. 'I was born in that house. I have lived all my life there. Now just let me die there,' she would plead.

But the nurses would just smile – there were so many like Emily in the unit, who seemed to lack the will to go on living. They gave her oxygen sessions and gradually she began to breathe more easily. Here at least they could be sure she took her tablets and medicine, which was rarely the case when she was at home. She began to eat again and the yellowy white pallor of her skin changed to a more natural tone. She even began to make friends with the others in the unit.

But the real change for Emily came one Saturday afternoon. A young girl came to the unit to play a flute. She was a slip of a girl and her playing was beautiful. Emily lay in bed and listened to the melodic sound. It touched her deeply and soothed her raw nerves. That night she slept soundly, far better than she had for years. The girl came again and the television was immediately switched off – something that rarely happened – and the patients listened in silence as the girl played. On that occasion Emily was out of bed sitting in a chair. She had always loved music, would have loved to have played an instrument, but when she was a young girl such a thing hadn't been possible.

The girl visited regularly and Emily and she became very friendly. She would sit and listen to Emily's stories and memories of her childhood. It did not matter that Emily repeated the same story many times, it was the telling that mattered.

Emily found the will to live again, and when the warmer weather came she moved back home. The neighbours were amazed – she looked so well. Every Tuesday and Thursday the ambulance would collect her for a visit to the unit, where she would have her hair done, chat to the other patients or play cards, and, of course, listen to the flute and chat to her new young friend.

That Christmas Emily received many presents. There were some lovely ones – warm sweaters, a box of groceries and chocolates. But none of them as lovely as a small silver model flute, which she placed with pride on the mantelpiece.

---

1 Collect photographs from magazines and newspapers which show old age. Make a display or collage out of them, adding your own poems and comments.

2 Find out about old people in your area. Are there ways in which you can help them? This could be done individually or as a class. If there are local representatives or organizations that help old people, invite them into school to talk to you.

3 Using a series of still pictures build up a series of events in the life of an old person.

Watching

Supposing a friend of yours does something you disapprove of, it could be something small or it could be something potentially dangerous. Do you try and stop them from doing it and risk losing their friendship?

The black limousines moved sedately past the quiet lawns and the rows of cedar trees, crawling steadily one behind the other, each keeping its discreet distance from the car in front. Frankie watched the slow, precise, controlled manoeuvre. Everything had been meticulously planned. There was not a single error, not one rash or unscheduled movement, nothing had been left to chance. It was difficult not to appreciate the irony of it all.

'Go on then,' Caroline demanded. That was a week ago, and she and Frankie were playing down by the canal. They always went down to the canal on a Saturday afternoon. They knew a spot near the old timberyard that was quiet. Private. Their place.

'Well, go on.' Caroline was standing on the bank opposite. Her jumper and jeans were dripping wet and water trickled from her long lank hair.

Frankie looked at the dark murky water. The canal was no longer used and the water was still, stagnant, dead.

'There's nothing to it,' Caroline shouted from the far bank. 'I did it in sixteen seconds. That's the record.'

'I'll get soaked. My mum'll kill me,' Frankie said.

'Don't be a baby.' Caroline was getting rather annoyed by now. 'You promised, Frankie. I've swum across, now it's your turn.'

'I can't,' Frankie replied feebly.

'Chicken!'

The cars came to a halt outside the small chapel. They formed a neat arc around the circular drive. Frankie watched as people got out. She moved out of sight as she saw Caroline's parents, both dressed unfamiliarly in black. The coffin was lifted from the lead car and carried into the chapel. Again, another smooth meticulous manoeuvre. Frankie would have liked to have followed the mourners into the chapel but she knew she couldn't. She was the last person they would want to see now.

'OK then,' Caroline said, 'if you're too chicken then don't.'

'It's not safe.'

Caroline scoffed. 'Tell you what, there's an old fridge dumped at the bottom. I saw it when I dived in. Bet there's something still inside. Let's take a look.'

'That's stupid,' Frankie called out. 'That's dangerous.'

Caroline laughed. 'What's wrong with danger?' And with that she dived back into the canal.

That was the last time Frankie ever saw her friend.

Frankie was confused about what had really happened; it seemed that the old fridge had tipped over when Caroline tried to open it, trapping the girl under its weight. Frankie knew she should have gone into the canal as soon as Caroline failed to resurface but in her panic it had never occurred to her to do so. By the time she had raised the alarm it was too late.

The mourners had all disappeared into the chapel. Everything was still and silent again. The only activity was a small group of men in black coats and hats, huddled together beside one of the limousines, talking quietly and lighting cigarettes.

Anyone could have crept up to the cars and let down the tyres without the men noticing. If only Caroline had been there – she'd have had a field day.

---

1 Discuss the following:

(a) What could Frankie have done to prevent the accident? Should she have gone into the water to try and rescue Caroline?

(b) Can you describe a dare that you have been involved in?

(c) Why do you think we make dares and challenges? Is there a fascination about danger? If so, what is it?

2 (a) Recreate the scene at the canal as told in this story. From there, see if the character of Frankie can think of strong arguments to dissuade Caroline from going into the water.

(b) Act out a meeting between Frankie and Caroline's parents.

3 As a group, sit yourselves in a circle. Someone is selected to begin, who turns to the person sitting next to him/her and issues a simple dare, e.g. 'I dare you to stand on your chair,' 'I dare you to sing the national anthem' etc. The next person must then add something to the first dare, thus making it more complicated. The challenge continues to be passed round the circle, getting more elaborate until one of the players feels it has got unreasonably difficult. At this point, he or she must say: 'It can't be done!' The dare-maker must then perform the dare and prove it can be done. If he or she succeeds, the person who said 'It can't be done' is out of the game. If the dare-maker fails to do the dare then the dare-maker is out. The game continues until there is only one person left in the circle.

After the game, discuss how the group behaved. Was the nature of the dares influenced by the fact that you might be challenged at any time to perform your suggestion? Was everyone prepared to perform the dares? Did anyone not say 'It can't be done!' because they didn't want to risk getting out?

Bernie in Love

Bernie meets the gorgeous Maddie and decides that being in love is not without its problems.

I think I'm in love.

I suppose it was bound to happen sooner or later. Life was all a bit too easy – everything ticking over nicely, the odd trauma here and there but by and large fairly trouble free. I suppose it was inevitable, knowing my luck, that something was going to crop up and throw everything into turmoil. Believe me, love plays havoc with your peace of mind.

Personally I blame Pincher Perkins. He is supposed to be my best mate, so when he invited me over last Sunday for a game of British Bulldog and a cream tea, he might at least have warned me. I didn't even know Pincher had a cousin, let alone that she would be there at his place all afternoon. I mean, he might have given me notice. 'By the way, Bern, I better warn you my cousin Maddie will be here on Sunday – she's a real cracker so for goodness sake don't turn up unless you're looking for trouble.' But no, Pincher said nothing. He let me walk right into it, like a lamb to the slaughter.

Maddie is the kind of girl that you dream about. How can I describe her? Words seem inadequate. She's like a cross between Helen of Troy and Princess Di. Her hair is golden as the sun, her skin as white as freshly fallen snow, her eyes as blue as the stripes on Queens Park Rangers' shirts, and she's got all her own teeth. When she smiled at me and said 'Hello' it took an enormous effort of will not to panic and hide behind the sofa. I tried to think of something suitably witty and erudite to say, but how do you impress someone who's perfect? So I just nodded and said 'Wotcher'. Not very earth shattering I'll admit, but at least contact had been made.

Pincher decided that trying to play British Bulldog with only the two of us was something of a non-starter, so instead he dug out his bat and a tennis ball and suggested french cricket instead. We're dead keen on french cricket, me and Pincher. It's a game of grace and elegance and as long as you don't stand too far away from the batter the ball's quite easy to catch. Tennis balls aren't as lethal as the real cricket variety and, though I say so myself, freed of the worry of broken fingers and split noses, I'm quite a fair old catcher. So when Pincher came downstairs bouncing a tennis ball on the floor I began to regain my composure. French cricket. Great! If anything was going to impress the beautiful Maddie this had to be it.

However, I hadn't banked on her joining in. I imagined she'd sit on the lawn watching and perhaps clapping genteelly at my display of dexterity. But when Pincher said, 'Who's in first?' Maddie grabbed hold of the bat. 'Ladies first, isn't it?' she declared. When Pincher asked her if she knew how to play she gave him the deadest eye this side of the mausoleum. Could she play? Put it like this, the game started at two fifteen. By the time we stopped for tea at three thirty-seven Pincher had been in twice, I'd been in once and Maddie had been in four times. At first we gave her a few easy throws. Her first two shots went over the fence and by the time he'd come back with the ball the second time Pincher had clearly decided to take off his kid gloves. He tried everything: the double take shot, the sly curler, the fast rolling-along-the-ground shot. But Maddie was equal to them all. She kept slogging at the tennis ball relentlessly. Even when she was caught out, the catches were deliberately easy ones, engineered as an act of charity. Believe me, if I hadn't already decided that I was passionately in love with her, I would certainly have felt humiliated.

After the game we had scones and jam. Then Pincher, who was still sulking over the french cricket fiasco, decided to escape to the sanctuary of his home computer. So then it was just me and Mads, as she likes to be known by her friends, just us two alone in the Perkins' back garden.

We didn't say much. Words were superfluous. I sat on the grass while she practised tennis shots against the back wall. Of course, there were loads of vitally important questions I wanted to ask – How old was she? Where did she live? What was her history teacher like? – but she was engrossed in hitting balls against the wall and who was I to disturb her?

In the end of course it got dark and I had to go home. I mean, in a way it was a bit of a disappointment – leaving. I thought about asking her if she wanted to go to the pictures next Wednesday, but it would've been a stupid reckless thing to do. I don't get my pocket money till Friday and even then it wouldn't stretch to two cinema tickets. However, we agreed to meet again. When I said, 'See you then', she smiled and said 'Yeh'. Can't be bad, eh? Actually, all in all, if it wasn't for the fact that I haven't been able to eat for three days and can't concentrate on my homework, I'd say being in love isn't as terrible as I'd expected it to be.

1 Discuss the following:
  (a) Do you think that Bernie has really discovered true love?
  (b) How do you think this relationship will develop?
  (c) What do you think Maddie's recollection of the afternoon will be?

2 Centre a group debate around the following statement: 'Falling in love is harder for men, because they have to take the initiative.' Consider whether you agree or disagree with this statement and give your reasons for and against.

3 In small groups act out one of the following:
(a) Two people meeting for the first time. The date has been arranged by 'Pot Luck Dating Agency'. They find that they are complete opposites of each other. How does the date progress?
(b) *The Photostory:* Think about the ingredients that go into a photo love story and see if you can create your own humorous version using freeze-frame images and 'voice over' captions.
(c) A girl comes down to breakfast one morning with a thick scarf round her neck. It's the middle of summer. What is she trying to hide, and how will her parents react to the situation?
(d) At a disco, a girl is being chatted up by a pushy boy whom she doesn't like much. He doesn't want to take 'no' for an answer. What can she do to get out of the situation?

WORK AND LEISURE
Bernie's Big Race

For Bernie, the chance to run in a school cross-country race is an unexpected challenge. Unfortunately the events of the race do not quite match his expectations.

Now I bet you've heard about kids who are good at everything – top in class, captain of sports, register monitor, prefect, proper all-round clever dicks. Me, I'm nothing like that. I'm just your ordinary sort of lad, not good not bad but average. Only I got a problem. Sports. Me and sports just don't get on. I'm keen enough but the problem is I'm not very good. You know when there's a gang of you going to play football and you pick out two captains and they take it in turns to name someone for their team and there's always one right wally left over at the end because neither team wants him? That's me. I'm the wally. Dead loss at sports I am.

I think I've worked out what the problem is – fear. Sports can be so dangerous. Take cricket for example: some lad does this impersonation of a windmill and then chucks half a hundred-weight of tightly-stitched leather at another lad holding a dirty great wooden stick who then wallops the ball as hard as he can in your direction. And what are you supposed to do? Run? Step out of the way? Phone the Red Cross? No – you're meant to go towards the ball and try to catch it. I mean, think about it, does that make sense? And if you don't try and catch it, Mr Jennings (he's our PE teacher) goes deep purple and starts calling you a 'lassie'. (I can't stand Mr Jennings – he's always looking for ways to make me look stupid. I reckon he only picks on me because I'm an easy target.)

Then there's rugby. Every winter at our school we have to play rugby. (We play rugby because everyone loves football and Mr Jennings is dead against people enjoying themselves.) Now rugby's OK if you're built like an ox with a neck the size of a tree trunk. Otherwise it's a non-starter. Worse than cricket. At least in cricket you only have one small ball to worry about. In rugby, some idiot hands you this oversized egg thing and before you know it half the third year's piled in on top of you like the Black Hole of Calcutta on a busy day. By the time the mass of arms, legs and boot studs have been untangled you're lucky if you get off with a broken collarbone. It's like organized gang warfare with points.

Mind you, I've developed a technique that's saved me many a broken bone on the rugby pitch. It works something like this: the minute you see someone in the same colour jersey running towards you with the ball you head off in the opposite direction, making it look like you're getting ready for a long cross-field pass when in fact what you're really doing is making sure there are at least half a dozen people between you and the ball at any one given moment in time. That way you're always miles from the action and your mum won't have to worry about getting bloodstains out of your shirt while still keeping to a low temperature on the washing machine.

As I see it, you don't need an A level in Brain Surgery to appreciate that sports like cricket and rugby are only designed to make you do one thing – hurt yourself. However, when I said I was a dead loss at sports it wasn't strictly true. Recently, I've discovered something that I'm not completely hopeless at – cross-country. We had this race a couple of months ago. It'd been snowing non-stop for four days so Mr Jennings decided it was time to send the whole third year out on a run. Last year we did a similar run and I came seventy-seventh out of a hundred – and even then if me and Pincher Perkins hadn't found a short cut I'd probably have done even worse. But this year I thought to myself – look Bernie, we've got a five-mile run here, there's a choice to be made: either you can walk round like last year and by the time you get back all the showers'll be full and some toe rag will have nicked your towel; or you can run, in which case you'll get back quicker and might even be home in time for *Grange Hill*. So I decided to give it a try. And would you believe it – I came tenth! Tenth out of a hundred! I suppose it must have been all that practice I had on the rugby field running away from the ball. To say I was chuffed would be an understatement. I thought about doing a lap of honour, but five miles is a long way when you stop and think about it.

I wasn't the only one who was pleased. Mr Jennings actually managed to say something nice. He came up to me and said, 'Well young Watts, at least you're not a complete write-off.' It was meant as a compliment, I think. Then he said, 'Keep it up. You might make the school team one day.'

The school team? Me? That'd be a turn up for the books. I spent the next two weeks hobbling up and down the school corridor (cross-country doesn't half rupture your leg muscles) waiting for my name to appear on the Cross-Country notice board. The team went up for the first race of the season, but my name wasn't on it. I wasn't picked for the second race either. But then, the following week it started to snow again and Mr Jennings, never one to look a gift horse in the mouth, arranged another third-year run. This time I actually finished fifth and when I looked at the notice board the next day there it was – Cross-Country Team: Watts, B. First Reserve. I didn't much like the sound of the First Reserve bit but I'd made it, I was in the team. My luck was really in because next day we heard that Lennie Collins, the team captain, had been rushed to hospital with suspected acute appendicitis. It was the best news I'd heard in ages. Mr Jennings put me in the first team and that night I sat down and wrote Lennie a thank-you note.

The day of the big race came. The race was taking place at our school but we still got off lessons early to get ready. You should've seen my maths teacher's face when I got up to leave. He couldn't believe someone like me would actually be running for the school, and when he found out it was true his face dropped a mile. He looked as if he'd just been sold an empty packet of Smarties.

There were twenty in the race all told, ten from each school. The other team looked a bit useful – most of them were bigger than us, though in cross-country that doesn't matter so much. We all got together and were told the route and then we were off. I sprinted out ahead of the rest as fast as I could. I knew it was my day. Today I just couldn't be beaten. The race started with three laps of the school field and by the end of the first lap I was twenty yards ahead of the rest.

By the second lap I was thirty yards ahead.

And by the third lap – six lads had already overtaken me. You see, I'd gone too quickly. Half-way through the third lap my legs just seemed to seize up. You know those dreams when you're trying to run away from something horrific but no matter how hard you try you just can't get moving – that's exactly how I felt. By the time we got to the school drive everyone seemed to be overtaking me: first Granger, then Latimer, then two lads from the other school, then three more, then Wallace, then Smith, then Harrison. Then the old caretaker pushing his wheelbarrow. I reckon even a snail could've beaten me into second place by that time. When I finally staggered out of the school gates and into the street all I could see was nineteen pairs of little legs disappearing into the distance. I was finished, caput, done for, and there was still another four miles to go. I ran the rest of the race all on my own, accompanied only by a few stray cats and an Alsatian with peculiar designs on my left leg. If only I hadn't sprinted at the start, if I'd hung in there with the rest of the main group, I might've done quite well. I might have come eighth or ninth, which would've been all right for a first race. But no, I had to go for broke, I had to do my Seb Coe impression. I made a complete jessie of myself.

That's what Mr Jennings said when I finally stumbled in forty-five minutes later. Everyone was showered and dressed and standing around drinking pop and cheering sarcastically (in between the laughter) as I zigzagged to the finishing post. 'Watts,' said Mr Jennings, 'you've made a complete jessie of yourself. I suppose we'd better call off the search party.' The other lads whooped with laughter and went home full of jovial witticisms.

When they'd all left I went to see Mr Jennings.

'You've let me down, Watts,' he said. 'You could have done much better than that.'

'They were too fast for me,' I explained.

'No boy, you were too fast for yourself. Pace, Watts. You have to be able to pace yourself. The way you dashed off at the beginning was ludicrous. You're not superman, you know. Go and get changed.'

I walked off towards the changing rooms, my head bowed, trying to look as pitiful as possible. My motto in life is don't feel sorry for yourself – just make sure everybody else feels sorry for you. Maybe it worked because just as I was going into the changing rooms Mr Jennings shouted my name.

'Yes, Sir?' I said, woefully.

'Make sure you do better next time,' he bellowed.

'Next time, Sir? I didn't think there'd be a next time.'

Mr Jennings smiled for the first time in his life. 'There's always a next time, Watts,' he said.

---

1 Discuss the following:

(a) Think about the last thing that Mr Jennings says: 'There's always a next time, Watts.' Can you explain what he meant by the remark and why he said it?

(b) How would you describe Mr Jennings as a teacher? Would you like to have him as one of your teachers?

(c) Can you remember any time when you thought something was going to be easy and it turned out to be difficult? How did you feel?

2 Think about the characters of Bernie and Mr Jennings and their relationship. In order to help you with this, agree amongst the group whose physical shape most resembles each of these two characters. Then take two larger sheets of paper – newsprint or lining paper would be ideal – and place them on the floor. The two volunteers lie down on the paper and their outline is drawn round carefully. The volunteers move away and all the pupils place phrases and words they associate with the characters on the paper, using felt-tip pens. Now discuss the words used. Remember the words relate to Bernie and Mr Jennings, not to the two volunteers.

3 In pairs act out a scene where Bernie comes home after the race and tells his mother and father *either* the truth of what happened in the race, *or* an untrue version in which he won the race. Then discuss the two versions. Which did you prefer? Which will be most helpful for Bernie in the future?

4 Act out a scene where over-confidence causes problems.

The Great Divide

Have you ever tried to form your own rock group? Sounds a good idea? It can be one of those projects that seem fine until the practicalities raise their ugly heads. 'The Great Divide' is a story about some friends in school who set up their own group, the problems they face and how they tackle them.

I found this guitar in our loft, quite old it was. Can't play it much but I decided then and there that I would start a rock group. I took the guitar to my mother and said, 'Look what I've found.' She threw a blue fit. I couldn't understand why. 'It'll keep me out of trouble,' I said. It turns out the guitar belonged to my dad. He left us when I was still in nappies. She asked me to put it back. After a real row I agreed, but I'm still going to start a group. Finding that guitar like that sort of made me want to do it.

A few weeks later and five of us had got it together. There was Dan on lead guitar, Brian on bass, Boz on drums and me and Jane on vocals. We called ourselves 'The Great Divide'. Smart don't you think?

Then came trouble. Boz was blasting us out on drums and he didn't like Jane. Next thing he stormed out taking Brian with him, just as we were getting started. So we're without a drummer and a bass. But it didn't stop us. We put up a notice at Dan's school: 'Wanted, bass player and drummer for group, must have own gear.'

Next day we had a new drummer, thirty teeny boppers wanting to be a star, but no bass. So what, we'll be a new sound without bass. We started rehearsing the new line-up and seemed to be making progress at last when we hit more problems. Dan didn't turn up to rehearse; someone said he'd got trouble with his girlfriend, then Archie the caretaker at the Welfare Hall wanted to boot us out. Making too much noise. We can carry on if we're quiet. 'How can you have a group playing without noise?' I asked him. But he didn't want to listen. I lost my cool and that caused more trouble.

From out of nowhere this guy appeared. Paid the caretaker a fiver, told us he'd be our manager and that our first booking is next week. Now hold on a minute, I said to myself. Terry, this can't be happening to you. But before we could think about it, Vince, that's our manager's name, got us to sign forms. Said he'd heard about us, liked the name 'The Great Divide' and that he was looking for new talent. We asked him about a bass and he said, 'No problem, you'll have one in a couple of days.' He didn't even want to hear us play but said he'd be in touch.

When Dan turned up half an hour later he threw a fit. 'How can we do a gig next week,' he said. 'We haven't even got a bass player!'

So we set about rehearsing the one song we knew, which we wrote ourselves. Here's a few lines from it:

'Stop, look, hear what we say,
Close your eyes and open your mind.
Stop, look, hear what we say,
We're sick and tired of being maligned.'

Well, we have only just started and we can't all be Paul McCartney.

We rehearsed for hours those next few days and learnt four songs. Vince sent us details of the gig and at last the day came. It was a reception at a wedding. 'They'll be too drunk to notice,' I thought to myself, more in hope than complaint.

We got there early, but not early enough. Who should be there but Boz and Brian and a few of their heavy-metal mates. We'd been double-booked. The heavy-metal blokes were making heavy noises and so we had no choice but to take our gear back down three flights of stairs and go home. Some gig. We tried to get in touch with Vince to sort it out but he had mysteriously disappeared. Now, I ask myself, do we carry on?

1 Think about different styles of pop music then prepare a short talk on the contribution your favourite group makes to the pop scene.

2 The story ends with the question: 'Do we carry on?' Discuss what advice you would offer to the group.

3 Divide into groups and choose a scene from the story to act out, such as the first rehearsal, or the first gig etc. See if you can develop the story in this way.

The Sands of Time

How do you feel about change? Do you welcome it or do you want things to remain the same? Do things always change for the better? If not – can you do anything about it?

Ever since I was born our family has gone camping for a week on the spring bank holiday. We always go to the same campsite in Wales which is very near the beach. For me it is the very best holiday I could have. Like us, other families have been coming for years and I know that I will meet the same group of friends. Mum says, 'The tents may change but the people don't.' When we all get together we swap stories about struggling with pushchairs on the cliff path down to the beach, wet days, sunstroke, jellyfish stings and losing bikini tops in the force of an extra big wave.

When we first came, the campsite was part of a typical Welsh farm. There were sheep in the field and you could buy eggs and milk at the farm. But the days of finding sheep in your tent are long since gone. Now the farmer makes his living out of pick-your-own strawberry fields, a trout lake and camping. The campsite has grown to twice its original size, with newly built showers and hot water. We could all have a game of rounders in the old days with the whole campsite taking part; now all you hear are radios blaring away, and even caravans with their own televisions.

When I'm in the tent at night and it's very dark I go over in my mind some of the very special memories of the camping holidays. There's the long car journey when just as you feel you can't stand it another minute, you arrive; putting up the tent, with Mum and Dad arguing like Laurel and Hardy:

'You've got it upside down!'
'It doesn't fit that way!'
'Look, I know what I'm doing!'

Then there was the time I upset chicken curry all over the tent floor. And the fear I felt when we had rats in the tent. And I'll always remember the sound of rain on the tent roof, catching tiny fish in rock pools and Dad playing french cricket. We always seem so much more of a family when we are camping. We have a barbecue on the beach each year and there are all the happy memories which go with that: wondering if it would light; stomach ache from too many burnt sausages; the late night swim; campfire songs; and most of all one time when I was very young. It was pitch dark after the brightness of the bonfire so we all held hands to make a human chain as we picked our way up the cliff path.

This year as usual we arrived in the pouring rain. We went straight down to the beach. Down the cliff path, past the swing on the tree. How many times have I been on that swing? The rain eased off and a shaft of sunlight cast its dazzle on the sea. The thought of a quick swim came into my mind. It was then that I noticed the thick brown film of oil on the water: pollution! When the tide went out a covering of sickly brown sludge could be seen in lines on the beach.

We didn't swim this year. That oil was there for the entire holiday. Dad says our camping days are over. Next year we will go to Spain – a cheap package, somewhere where we can rely on the sun.

I won't go. I don't know what I shall do.

When I was unpacking after the holiday I found that the tent pockets were still full of sand. I picked up a few grains and watched them trickle through my fingers. Something came into my mind – it was the words from an old song I had learnt at junior school: 'The sands of time have run out.'

1 Discuss the following:

(a) Which kind of holiday do you prefer: camping or staying in a hotel? In Britain or abroad?

(b) What do you think Helen meant when she said: 'We always seem so much more of a family when we are camping'? Is there an activity or a time when you feel your family is closer?

(c) Is it too risky for young people to go on holiday without their parents?

(d) Should people hitch-hike?

2 Divide the class into two groups: one group work for the tourist board of a British coastal resort; the other group are representatives of a holiday complex abroad, e.g. Majorca. Devise ways of persuading people to come to your holiday centre. Then take it in turns to try and persuade your teacher to come to your resort.

3 Try to recall incidents that happened when you were younger. They could be happy or sad times but should be ones that you would be confident in sharing with your friends. In small groups take turns to retell the incident in as interesting a way as possible. You may wish to tape-record them.

Beep Click

Do you use computers at school? If you do, are you aware of the many ways in which they can help you to learn? As well as the advantages in having computers, however, there are also disadvantages, and this story shows one of them. Barry is fourteen and spends most of his spare time playing games on his computer.

I like to shoot 'em up – aliens, enemies, space bugs and aircraft. If you don't wipe them out, they will destroy you. And that means the game is over and you have to start all over again. It's that feeling of your finger on the fire button – you feel in control, you feel powerful. Computer games are a test of skill, a complex human being matched against a complex machine. Most times the odds are stacked against you and the machine wins. At other times you reach the highest level and complete the game and then it's magic.

There's another kind of rivalry too, that's between you and your mates. It's to see who can get a new game first, then the first one to complete it. Once that's done, you swap it for a different game. Games are coming out each day and nobody wants the old ones. I spend all of my pocket money on my computer and even that's not enough to try out all the games.

When I'm in my bedroom with the computer I forget about homework, kid sisters and parents. I'm in a world of my own. Time and day don't matter. You just flick on the switch and you're there, dodging bullets, laser beams and baddies. You wait for those seconds to pass by as the programme is loading, watch as the waving lines pass by on the screen and the buzzing whine stops. Then you read 'Press any key to start' and your heart misses a beat and you're into the fantasy world of the computer game.

Barry's mum, however, feels very differently about the computer.

It's a beautiful sunny day today and what is he doing? That's right, playing on that computer. When we bought it for him for Christmas the man in the shop said it was 'an essential learning agent in the new age of technological advance.' But all he does is play games on it.

We want him to do well in the future and have a good job, and buying him a computer seemed the right thing to do. You hear so much about them these days, don't you? Banks use them, so do industry and big organizations. Barry said we could do our household accounts on it, but we haven't bothered.

If Barry can't load in a game or has trouble with it he's miserable and bad-tempered for the rest of the day. He spends all his pocket money on the silly things as well. Last week he had just saved up £10 to go towards his holiday and what does he do? Goes and spends it all on a game, then can't load it in. He and his mates copy each other's games and it was in the paper only yesterday that a copy squad fined someone £1,500 for doing just that.

We've tried to stop him playing on his computer, but that only causes more trouble. I really don't know what to do next.

1 Discuss the following:
   (a) With the person next to you, talk about how Barry feels and why you think he spends so much time with his computer. Then report your ideas to the class. Do these ideas tell you any more about Barry and his use of the computer?
   (b) How do you feel about computer games? Are they harmless?
   (c) Do you think young people are exploited by computer game manufacturers?
   (d) How do computers affect your life? Can you list the different ways?

2 Imagine you are the advertising department of a computer games firm. Either in small groups or as a whole class invent a new game to be launched on the market. You could design a logo for the game. Role play a meeting where you discuss your campaign to launch the new game. Who are you selling to? What will appeal to them? How much will you charge for the game? How can you make sure it will sell well?

Super Gran

Does it really matter how old people are? Do you have to be young to be fit and athletic? What age do you think of as being old? Can you remember when you felt too old for a particular situation? 'Super Gran' pushes aside her age in an attempt to prove that people are never too old. This description of 'Super Gran' is given by Lisa who is thirteen.

I know a lot of grans who are boring. They are always moaning, saying how ill they feel or that kids today are too noisy, scruffy and cheeky. Weren't they ever young once? Didn't they want to enjoy themselves?

But my gran's not like that. She's great is my gran. She lets me stay up to watch telly when she's looking after me, when Mum and Dad have gone out.

In fact we call her 'Super Gran'. Why? Because she runs races. That's right, she runs races. She told me that she's sixty-four. Now that seems old to me. But you wouldn't think my gran was old. Every morning and night she goes jogging. It began by just going round the street and back but now she runs miles and miles. Sometimes I go with her. I quite like jogging. Sometimes I want to stop and have a rest but Gran doesn't want to stop. I think she goes slowly sometimes just so I can keep up. When we start off I'm the one at the front but after a bit I'm starting to lag behind and Gran is slowing down for me. You wouldn't believe that would you? I'm only thirteen and she is sixty-four, but she can run so much better than me.

About a year ago she really started to take the running seriously. She ran in a fun run – I think it was thirteen miles. Mum and Dad got very worried about her. 'You ought to be getting your feet up,' they said. 'Why don't you stick to knitting or reading? You'll do yourself no good with this running!' But Gran wouldn't listen. She said that she was old enough to look after herself. And anyway, she'd never felt better.

One time I was walking home from school with my mates when Gran came jogging past in her pink jogging outfit. She waved at me as she went past. 'Who's that weirdo?' asked one of my mates. When I said that it was my gran they started to laugh and make fun of me. But I don't care. I'm really proud of my gran.

After the fun run Gran really started to change. Every Saturday night we go up to the club for a night out. Mum and Dad and Gran would have a few drinks and enjoy themselves. One week Gran didn't come and she has not been since. She's stopped eating meat and she eats this special food – lots of nuts and raisins. Mum and Dad said she was going crazy, but I didn't think so. Then she hurt her leg. I don't know how it happened but she finished up in hospital with the leg in plaster. 'That will put a stop to her running,' said Mum.

Did it? It did not. The plaster was off in two weeks and she was back running. I heard Dad say, 'Where will it end? Where will it end?'

Then Gran entered for the London Marathon. Everybody said that was the last straw. But I didn't. I really thought Gran could do it. I'd got faith in her even if nobody else had.

You see, some time ago I went to Gran's to watch the London Marathon on television with her. She sat glued to that set all day. She couldn't take her eyes off it. That's not like Gran. Normally she's not bothered about watching television. I remember we saw one old man of eighty finish the race in five hours twenty-six minutes.

'If he can do it, then so can I,' said Gran, and she meant it. 'My mother jumped up and down on a pogo stick on her sixtieth birthday. "I'll show them," she said. And so will I.'

Now you know why I call her 'Super Gran'.

Show us she did, for that spring, sure enough, Gran was to take part in the London Marathon. We travelled down with her to London. A bus was arranged for us to go round the course the day before. We had been on the bus two hours and still not got to the finish. We didn't say anything but I'm sure that we all thought that Gran had no chance, it seemed such a long way, and the furthest she'd run was fourteen miles.

None of us slept that night but at last the day arrived. We got up very early, half-past five I think it was. We had to catch a train and then a tube. Even at that time there were crowds around. We were to see her start, then travel to the finish. It was a beautiful sunny day and everyone seemed very excited. You could sense one single purpose that had brought us all to this one place at the same time. It seemed a real relief when at last the race started. Gran was near the back next to a man dressed up as a Viking. Not only did he have horns on his head but a ship made out of cardboard round his waist!

The gun fired but nobody seemed to move. Everybody was so jam-packed together it seemed impossible for them to walk let alone run. At last they began to shuffle, then trot, and at long last Gran broke into a run. We all cheered and moved off to go to the finishing line.

Time passed and as we waited there for Gran to finish the sun grew hotter and hotter. Runners were finishing all the time but still no sign of her. Some runners looked quite fit but most were exhausted. I have never seen people look so hot and sweaty. One old man collapsed on the finishing-line itself. Poor old Gran, I thought, where is she now? Then I had a strange feeling that she had had an accident and she was perhaps even dead. I just wanted to get away and go home. 'Gran, I shall never see you again,' I said to myself.

Then at last I could see her. She'd taken her tracksuit off and I could see her yellow T-shirt with 'Super Gran' printed across the front. I felt so proud. The next moment she had crossed the line and someone wrapped her in a blanket and put a medal around her neck. Before I knew what I was doing I was running up to her and kissing her.

When it was all over Gran said, 'Without doubt this has been the most fantastic day in my life.' She speaks for me too.

---

1 Discuss the following:
  (a) How would you feel if your gran was a 'Super Gran'? Would you be too embarrassed to tell your friends?
  (b) Is it too risky for older people to take part in a sport?
  (c) Imagine you had been asked to plan a home for the elderly. What facilities would you provide for them?

2 Organise the class to role play the board of a sports team, such as soccer, rugby, hockey etc. Your team lacks spirit and enthusiasm. You have a vacancy for a new player. Get two people to take the roles of applicants to join the team. One is young and fit, the other is old and fit and is very keen to play for your team. Interview them and make your selection. Then say why you chose the person you did.

Invaders

Have you been really frightened by something that you have seen on television, or a very scary film? This is what happened to Elizabeth after a visit to the cinema.

We were on holiday in the Yorkshire Dales at the time. It was in November, a wet day, and being bored we went to the cinema. It meant a thirty mile drive, but Mum and Dad said it would cheer us up. The film was called *The Invaders*. Now I hate horror films, but Dad loves them. I don't know why he tried to pretend that it was for my benefit we were going to the pictures, but con us he did. I closed my eyes during most of it, and all I could see when I took a peep was masses of green slime, always green slime and weird creatures. I was glad when it was over.

We were staying at an old cottage for the week which had a really creepy atmosphere. It was over two hundred years old and was just the sort of place that could be haunted by a ghost. That night I couldn't get off to sleep, my mind seemed full of pictures of weird creatures and green slime.

I must have drifted off to sleep at last. Suddenly I woke up. It was pitch black and very quiet. I could just hear the wind blowing through the trees outside. I didn't know at first what had made me wake up. Then I heard it, a faint shuffle from the other side of the bedroom partition, which formed part of the kitchen of the cottage. The noise came again. There was someone there. I could definitely hear breathing. It couldn't be Mum or Dad, could it? The breathing was like a sort of snorting. I was rigid. It was so black. I was breathing through my mouth. My heart was beating right into my head. I cried out. The movements stopped. The invader must be listening too. Then the breathing and moving started again. It didn't sound human. Was I really awake or was I dreaming? Then there was a crash as some bottles were knocked over.

I had read about things like this in the paper. I could see the headlines: 'Invaders wipe out family. Brave defence by twelve-year-old girl. Posthumous medal to be presented. Interview with distraught next of kin.'

My heartbeat got louder. The noise grew, the snorting and snuffling filled the room. There must be more than one. 'I've got to do something,' I said to myself. To get out of the room I had to go through the place where the creatures were. Could I do it? 'You idiot,' I said to myself. 'Put the light on. The most obvious thing and you haven't even thought of it.' My hand fumbled for the light switch. It was only then that I realized the lightbulb had blown and we hadn't replaced it.

Crash! Over went some more bottles. Now what? I could hear Dad cursing. But try as I might I couldn't call out, I was just too scared. Then I saw a glimmer of light. It was Dad coming with a torch. 'What's the trouble, Elizabeth?' he asked. Somehow I managed to say, 'In there.' Dad took me by the hand and the light from his torch caught the shambles in the kitchen. Bottles and jars lay strewn over the floor. A bottle of milk had been tipped over and a puddle of milk oozed from it. Slurping up the milk was a hedgehog. It didn't even seem to notice that we were there. It was snorting and snuffling and scratching at a polythene bag which also lay on the floor. It was the biggest hedgehog you've ever seen. So much for invaders. Dad gathered the polythene bag around it and carried it out into the garden. But how had it got in? The cottage had remained empty for some weeks but it was still a mystery.

The very next night I woke up abruptly in the very same way. Just the same blackness. I lay there thinking and listening for any strange sounds. There weren't any; just a powerful silence. I couldn't get back to sleep and my mind turned to the animal invader and I wondered where the hedgehog might be at that very moment. In a strange kind of way I felt that we were the invaders in the cottage, renting it for just a few short days, then going back to our neat little bungalow, and that perhaps the hedgehog had more right to be there than we did.

---

1 Discuss how many of you regularly watch horror videos. Are they harmless? Do they affect the way people behave?

2 Sit or lie in a space by yourself, away from the rest of the group. Imagine you are alone and frightened. It might help to recall a past experience of a similar nature. Where do you imagine yourself to be? What time of day is it? What has made you scared? Quietly speak your thoughts and feelings aloud.

3 Get the class to sit in a circle. Now try to create a scary story together, with each person in turn adding a word or a phrase. For example, you could start with: 'It was so dark I couldn't even see my hand in front of me . . . ' Your story could be serious or funny. However, try to agree on the mood and keep to it.

The Pennine Way

> *The Pennine Way is a two-hundred-and-fifty mile walk along the Pennine hills and stretches from the Peak district of Derbyshire to the borders of Scotland. Hugh is a nineteen-year-old lad who has just completed the walk.*

It all began when I saw a blind lady being guided round the hypermarket where I work. A strange way to begin you might think but my friend Vince told me that it costs over £700 to train a guide dog for the blind. So Vince and I decided to do a sponsored walk of the Pennine Way. Not that I'd done much walking before. In fact I thought the idea was crazy but Vince got us organized.

First we had to train for fitness. That meant jogging. Not just ordinary jogging, but running with a rucksack full of bricks on your back. I know what you're thinking – crazy! – just what I thought. Then we had to harden our feet by soaking them in some purple chemical. Mine came out like pickled walnuts. Finally, we had to pack our gear. I even had to cut the handle off my toothbrush to save on space and weight.

At last we were ready. It was going to take us two weeks and we had just enough time in our summer holiday. Leaving Edale in Derbyshire, we climbed up a very steep moor called Jacob's Ladder. The view was breath-taking. Vince is a keen footballer and very fit but I felt terrible. We had only come two miles and had over twenty to walk the first day.

Then came the rain. The skies opened and it poured. The clouds came down and so did the mist. You could barely see a few metres ahead. We lost our way and stumbled about in the middle of nowhere. Vince took a compass reading and on we trundled. I can honestly say that I have never felt so miserable. The hours passed and we were both soaked to the skin. At last it was time to stop for the night. We had a primitive lean-to tent and crawled in for the night. All we had to eat was one tin of cold baked beans between us. The rain had soaked our matches and we could not light our stove to cook anything. What a foul, miserable, shivering night.

It rained all night. I was ready to give up, but Vince was determined to continue. We packed all the gear and off he set expecting me to follow. What should I do? Follow Vince or turn back and find a bus back home? There seemed no choice. On I went.

At last it stopped raining and things improved. That night we stopped in a youth hostel. What bliss! A warm bed and hot food; life was almost bearable.

Soon we reached the Yorkshire Dales and I began to enjoy myself.

Perhaps that fitness training was paying off. The scenery was spectacular – Malham Cove and Tarn, Gordale Scar, Penyghent – if you've never seen these places you really ought to visit them.

It was after the Yorkshire Dales that Vince began to have trouble with his knee. Earlier he had blisters on his heel and had to walk in an awkward fashion. That put pressure on his knee and he began to limp. By the time we had reached Hadrian's Wall it was really a problem. One day we walked only eight miles and we needed twice that distance to keep to our timetable. We had covered two hundred and ten miles, just forty left. We rested the night and hoped for the best.

The next morning the knee was rigid and Vince couldn't walk at all. It looked as if the walk was over. We looked at the map and estimated that it was about two miles to the nearest road. I volunteered to give Vince a piggyback over the two miles, leave the rucksacks where we were and then collect them on a return journey. Vince agreed after some persuasion. He was just about in tears. How our roles had changed from that first day of the walk! Now I was the leader.

That two miles was sheer hell. Vince stumbled some of the way on his own and I carried him the rest. I left him on a ridge just overlooking the road and returned for the gear. I felt very disappointed that we had to call it a day but my main concern was to get Vince to civilization. As I neared the ridge with the rucksacks I heard Vince shouting out that a bus was coming along the road. I thought he had cracked up. A bus in the middle of nowhere! But it was true. Exhausted as I was, I ran to the road, shouting and waving my arms as I went. The driver saw me and the bus came to a halt.

Some time later we were both on the bus and the driver kindly loaded the gear in the boot. As I sat there a phrase came into my mind. It was from the Pennine Way guidebook: 'If you start, don't give up, or you will be giving up at difficulties all your life.' Before I knew it I was on my feet and asking the driver to unload my rucksack. I had decided to go on alone. With apologies to Vince I climbed out of the bus. I shall never forget the look on Vince's face gazing out of the window as the bus drew off and passed me. 'Now, Hugh,' I said to myself, 'you are on your own.'

I finished the walk two days later. The last day I walked twenty-nine miles. I surprised myself. I don't see much of Vince these days. The walk has meant the end of our friendship. My success was at a cost. But somewhere right now a blind person has a guide dog of their own, and our walk made that possible.

---

1 Discuss the following:
   (a) Why do you think Hugh says, 'I don't see much of Vince these days'? Why do you think the relationship between the two lads changes so much during the walk?

(b) Try and remember times when you have: given up easily at the first sign of difficulty and/or persevered and completed a task despite real problems.

2 Imagine you are setting up a sponsored event – disco, walk, swim etc. Decide as a class what the event is and to whom the money is to be given. Discuss what practical arrangements you need to make. Then in small groups make up a commentary for the event. It could be taped, written or spoken.

3 The imaginary event is now over. Divide into three groups and tackle one of the following:
(a) Some sponsorship money is missing. Discuss what should be done about it.
(b) Act out the presentation of the money you have collected.
(c) Prepare a newspaper article or local television item about the event.

The Protest

Most of us have opinions and beliefs that influence the way we are and the lives we lead. In this story a matter of principle leads to a new way of life.

Something happened to my father a short while ago. He gave up his job. I suppose there's nothing unusual in that – hundreds, maybe thousands, lose their jobs every day of the year. But the circumstances under which my father gave up his job are different. He was working in a scientific laboratory where they test new products. It was very well paid and we enjoyed a comfortable life – holidays abroad, two cars, video recorders, that sort of thing. However, during the last year Dad's work in the laboratory changed. He became involved in testing various new perfumes on animals.

Dad didn't like the idea from the start and asked not be involved in it. He was told he would have to do the work for a short while, until they were able to find someone else and move him to another project. Given the circumstances, he felt he had no choice but to agree and so he took part in the experiments.

The scientists bred special rats and sprayed the perfume on them. Dad didn't say much about his work, just that 'It's a job.' But he became very quiet, not at all his usual cheery self. He and Mum began to have long talks. Apparently the perfumes had terrible effects on the rats. Exactly what, Dad never said. Despite these results the work continued. It was called 'controlled experimentation' and had to last for several weeks if the findings were to be valid. They varied the amount of spray and the rats' diet, but the terrible results continued.

Weeks went by and Dad thought the experiments were at an end. But then a new series of tests was planned, with a modified perfume and more rats. Dad had had enough but they insisted that since he had been in charge of the first experiments he had to organize the second. That was it, he'd had doubts all along but he refused to involve himself further. He resigned on the spot. They were shocked.

'But Mr Harris,' he was told, 'you have worked here for many years. A scientist does not become personally involved, he remains objective about his work. You have always appreciated that, surely?'

'I have my principles,' my father told them.

'Yes Mr Harris, and we're pleased you do. But in these difficult financial times the laboratory has to take on new and expanding work.'

'Does it?' said Dad. 'Well, it can do it without me.'

He told us the whole story and we felt very proud of him – our Dad putting his principles first. We all agreed that he had done the right thing and if it had been any of us we hoped we would have done exactly the same.

Dad wrote a letter to the newspapers about his protest, but they didn't print it. They had more important things to put into print, like fashion models and advertisements for the latest perfumery.

Dad was lucky, he wasn't without a job for long. He now works in a health food shop. It's far less money and this year we won't have that holiday abroad. But at least he is happy. I don't ever remember seeing him so relaxed. He's joined various organizations to protect animal rights and it's made us all think about how animals are treated. As a family we feel that experiments involving animals should be banned by law. What do you think?

---

1 Discuss to what extent scientific experiments involving animals are justifiable. Should there be a blanket ban? What restrictions would you impose on scientists?

2 Choose one member of the group to play Mr Harris. The rest of the group assume the role of the committee of an animal rights' organization. Before the group accept him into their organization Mr Harris must justify his reasons for taking part in the initial experiments at the laboratory and explain why he took so long to resign his post.

3 Draw up your own list of dos and don'ts i.e. the things that you believe are right or wrong. As a group, compare the lists and consider what principles, if any, are common to the whole group. Then discuss why you think as you do, e.g. do you think something is right or wrong because your teachers or parents think it is right or wrong?

The Hollywood Dream

We all have dreams and ambitions. Sometimes, it's hard to tell the difference between a dream and a realistic aspiration. In this story the central character has a dream that he believes he can achieve.

Baxter Bogart wanted to be a movie star.

'I mean, I've got the name haven't I?' he used to tell his friends. 'And that always helps.' He worked as a doorman at the Royale Cinema. 'I believe every job should have prospects,' he told the proprietor at his interview. 'If a job hasn't got prospects it isn't worth doing, that's what I say.' He took the job because of its prospects. Everybody had to start somewhere and Baxter saw the Royale as an ideal starting-point for his career in motion pictures. The proprietor took him on at once – he knew when he was on to a good thing.

Baxter quite enjoyed life as a doorman but after a while he began to grow disenchanted. He had been at the Royale for nearly fifteen years. At times he felt they were fifteen years of his life wasted. He was nearly forty. Fifteen years he had stood outside the Royale, ushering people in, offering advice – 'Screen Two's a good 'un this week; I don't recommend Screen Three, all blood and guts' – and occasionally escorting drunken young men from the premises. Of course, it was a living, and he was entitled to free tickets on his day off, but nevertheless Baxter decided that the time had come to make his move. Accordingly, he booked an appointment to see the proprietor to discuss future prospects.

Baxter knocked at the office door.

'Come in,' shouted the cinema proprietor.

Baxter entered. The proprietor looked up from behind his small, paper-strewn desk.

'Oh it's you Bogart,' he said without enthusiasm.

'I hope you don't mind me barging in sir.'

'Well Bogart, what do you want?'

Baxter paused, took off his cap and tucked it neatly under his arm. 'Future prospects, sir. I want to discuss my future prospects.'

'You're not having a pay rise,' the proprietor said sharply.

'I don't want a rise, sir. The thing is I . . . well, what I mean . . . ' Baxter hesitated, stumbled for the right words. All at once his plans to move on seemed to smack of ingratitude and disloyalty.

The proprietor grew impatient. There was an awkward pause.

'I'm not very happy sir,' Baxter said in a loud sudden voice.

'Oh, I'm sorry to hear that Bogart.' The proprietor smiled sympathetically. 'Do sit down.'

'Do you think that will help, sir?'

'Sit down.'

'Yes, sir. Thank you, sir.' Baxter Bogart sat down.

'Now then Bogart, what are you unhappy about?'

'Basically sir, it's my job.'

'You're not happy in your work?'

'Not really, sir.'

'And what exactly are you unhappy about?' asked the proprietor. 'Would you like a new uniform, or something like that?'

'No, sir. I'm quite happy about the uniform but it's the . . . future prospects, you see.'

'What future prospects are those?'

'Well,' Baxter said firmly, 'I think it's time I moved on. I mean, as you know, it's my ambition to be a movie star. Why are you smiling, sir?'

'Nothing in particular,' the proprietor replied, trying to stifle a giggle. 'You want to be a film actor, is that what you're saying?'

'Yes, sir. After all, I've got the name and that always helps.'

'Yes, of course.' The proprietor got up and went to a small window. Outside it was getting dark. The patrons would soon be arriving, to be greeted as ever by the cheery smile of the theatre doorman. Often people had complimented the proprietor on the excellent service of the staff, and Baxter Bogart was indeed an example to all with his quiet smile and good manners. In fact, thought the proprietor, one might almost call him irreplaceable. He turned suddenly from the window. 'Tell me, Bogart,' he said, 'this name of yours – is it real?'

'Well, sir, more or less.'

'In other words it isn't.'

'I used to be called Bloggard sir. But then I decided Bogart sounded better. After all, Humphrey made it didn't he? And so did his cousin Dirk.'

'Nevertheless, Bogart, think of the thousands and millions of Bogarts who weren't so lucky. Tell me, how do you plan to get into the movie business.'

'Well, sir,' Baxter said, twisting his cap nervously, 'I'm thinking about going to Hollywood.'

'Where?' the proprietor said.

'Hollywood sir, in America. I think there are better openings there, better prospects for a movie star. Not that the prospects at the Royale are bad, but I'm not sure I'll ever be a movie star if I stay here.'

The proprietor took a large cigar from his breast pocket. He lit up, leaned against the side of his small desk and drew heavily on the cigar. After much thought he said: 'Look here Bogart, I'll be perfectly frank with you. I know you're serious about this film acting business but, well, I don't know if I can afford to let you go.'

'But sir –'

'Let me finish, Bogart. If you were to leave us we would be hard pressed to find a suitable replacement.'

'But, sir,' Baxter said, feeling rather guilty as he did so, 'I don't want to seem ungrateful but being a cinema doorman gets rather boring after a while.'

'Of course, I understand that.' The proprietor nodded understandingly. 'Tell you what, Bogart, I'm prepared to do a deal with you.'

'What sort of deal, sir?'

'I'd be prepared to let you go off to Hollywood as long as you promise to stay at the Royale until we've found a suitable replacement.'

Baxter considered the request carefully. On the one hand, he was desperately keen to get to Hollywood as soon as possible and make his big break in the movie world. But on the other hand, it was obvious that the Royal cinema needed his services. As the proprietor rightly said, a good doorman is hard to find these days. 'Very well then, sir,' he said finally. 'I'll stay until you've found someone to replace me.'

The proprietor shook Baxter warmly by the hand. 'Good man, Baxter. I'm sure it will only take a couple of months to find the right person, and then you can go off and find your fortune.'

'Thank you, sir.' Baxter grinned proudly.

'Now then,' the proprietor said, looking at his watch, it's about time for the evening house. You'd better get down there Bogart, your public is waiting for you.'

'Yes indeed, sir.' Baxter put on his cap, with some pride, and marched briskly out of the office.

The proprietor sat down behind his desk and puffed at his cigar. Bogart was a strange type really, not at all like the other attendants and usherettes. He was a unique man in many ways. He took great pride in his work as though being the doorman at a provincial cinema was an artform in itself. Bogart was the last of a rare breed – reliable, thoughtful and above all loyal. And yet, thought the proprietor, it was strange that they still had this same discussion every year. Bogart had been doorman at the Royale since that rainy day in May, fifteen years ago, when he had turned up at the theatre in reply to the proprietor's advertisement in the local paper. Fifteen long years ago. And since then, every year, on the first day of May, Bogart came to the office to discuss his future prospects, his dreams of Hollywood and movie fame.

The proprietor leaned back in his chair. He wondered if Bogart ever would get to Hollywood and if he would be happy if he did. Yes, Baxter Bogart was an odd type. And, certainly, he was the best cinema doorman that the Royale had ever employed. It would be wrong to re-advertise the position. Very wrong indeed.

---

1 Discuss the following:
   (a) Do you think Baxter really believes in his 'Hollywood dream'? What prevents him from realising his dream?
   (b) Is the proprietor wrong not to re-advertise Baxter's post? Why do you feel he wants to stop Baxter leaving? Are doormen really so hard to find?
   (c) How important is it to have dreams? Is there a difference between dreams and ambitions?
   (d) In a perfect world, what would you most like to be, or do?

2 In small groups, act out one of the following situations:
   (a) A group of contestants backstage at a talent contest. Show how you feel they would behave towards each other as they take turns to go off and do their act.
   (b) A chat show host interviewing two 'celebrities'. What kind of questions might be asked?
   (c) Consider any weird dream or nightmare that you can remember having and see if you can think of an effective way of re-enacting it. This could involve use of sound effects, lighting and music.
   (d) The story of an 'ordinary' person who wakes one day to find that a dream has come true (e.g. winning the pools, getting the perfect job etc). How does the good fortune affect the person's life and the lives of those around him/her?

Snowman

Have you ever been in a situation where a joke backfires? Or perhaps a dare that is particularly dangerous? In this story a seemingly harmless bit of fun almost has tragic consequences.

The trouble with snow is that it doesn't last long enough. You wake up one morning and it's snowing and you think, Great – no school today, we'll be blocked in by six–foot drifts and won't be able to open the front door. Your eyes start to water and you almost cry at the prospect of missing a day at school. Know what I mean?

Just as you think that, the white flakes stop and out comes the sun and your dreams of a day at home in front of the telly or in bed have, like the snow, faded away. Or, there's a really good covering during the evening and you think, Great – can't wait until tomorrow. And you wake up next morning and all the snow has gone, as if some thief has run off with it in the night and hidden it where you can't find it.

Sometimes the prospect of a good snowball fight almost makes the prospect of turning up at school at ten to nine bearable. On those days the lessons just get in the way of the real business of the day and you spend your time in class looking at your watch and drying out your clothes before the next thrilling instalment of seeing which teacher you can snowball at breaktime.

One time we had a competition to see who could land the most snowballs on any teacher. The caretaker or dinner ladies didn't count, only teachers. If you hit the deputy head that counted double, if you got the head – winner takes all. Only trouble was that the head never set foot outside.

Yesterday it snowed for the first time this winter. It was amazing to see all the kids who hadn't been to school for ages suddenly appear at the school gates. One lad who was supposed to be ill with a serious disease suddenly made a miraculous recovery. Of course there's wimps, who don't come 'cause they're scared of getting a few snowballs lobbed at them. We all know who they are. Their mums give them a note for the next day: 'Sorry Jeremy wasn't at school yesterday, he had hay fever.' Hay fever? In the middle of January?

Anyway, I was standing in the school drive and I saw the head walking towards me and I thought: I could win the jackpot if I land one on him. But if he gave me a hard stare and shouted: 'You boy, put that snowball down!'

My grip loosened around the snowball and it fell to the ground.

Just then there was a shriek of laughter from the corner of the drive. A school window had been left open and Lucy Headstock had just lobbed a snowball in. The deputy head sent for her and, guess what? You've guessed it. She was let off – just because she's a girl.

I spent the day standing by radiators and snowballing. Four o'clock came and a whole gang of us were down the road snowballing. Teacher's cars were scuttling through the barrage. I threw along with the rest. Suddenly a car swerved and a little kid was knocked off her bike.

A crowd gathered, the snowballers stopped. An ambulance was sent for while the small girl lay motionless in the road. No longer funny, no more jokes.

Today we heard that Tracy is all right, so the story didn't end in tragedy, though her bike is smashed. But next time, Tracy or Clare or Robert, or whoever, might not be so lucky.

1 Does your school have rules about snowballing? If so, discuss if you think they are sensible. If not, make up your own set of rules.

2 Design a poster or invent a television commercial warning people of the dangers of snowballing in the street.

3 Act out a scene where a seemingly harmless bit of fun ends in tragedy.

Bernie's Report

Bernie has a strong dislike for school reports, especially when they don't reflect his own judgement of how he feels he has done. But what if pupils could write reports about their teachers?

This is not a good time for me. Last Friday Mr Duncan came into the classroom carrying a stack of envelopes under his arm and a broad smirk across his face. You didn't need to be Sherlock Holmes to figure out what was up. School reports.

You can always tell when the school report is due. Teachers can be seen gazing furtively around the class and then scribbling hurried notes in their ledger books. Kids like Dirty Davidson, who normally wouldn't recognise hard work if it kicked them in the shins, start putting their hands up in class and handing their homework in on time. Nobody says boo to a goose when the school report is due.

The reports themselves seem to follow the same inevitable pattern. Last year's 'Fair progress' might become this year's 'Reasonable improvement'; otherwise it's all pretty much of a muchness. As usual, according to my teachers, I'm something of a disappointment. Apparently I am not without potential but my progress is 'erratic' (what does that mean?) and I lack self-will. 'This boy contents himself with mediocrity', as the headteacher, Mr D.T. Hubble commented at the bottom of my report. I haven't seen Mr Hubble outside of school assembly since the start of the first year so I'm somewhat baffled as to how he felt qualified to make any comment at all. Least said soonest mended I would have felt. Still, it's done now.

My mother was less than happy with my showing. My father said little but from the look on his face I don't think he was overjoyed either. As per usual, my school report proved something of a washout. Not that I'd have been too concerned if I'd expected to do badly. But I was convinced I'd done quite well this year. I mean, how can you get B+ for practically every piece of written work in English and still wind up with a 'C−, could do better' on your report? I wouldn't be surprised if I'd been mixed up with Charlie Watts of 3H. Charlie comes bottom at everything given half a chance.

Well I have decided, I'm not taking this lying down. Two can play at this game. I'm going to get my own back. Tomorrow morning the following report sheet is going to appear on the school noticeboard:

Biology: Mr Evans still needs to put more enthusiasm into his work. He is capable of speaking eloquently and at great length about the majesty of the Pontypridd forward line but seems to have only a passing interest in the subject he is supposed to be teaching. Greater commitment is needed in the coming year.

Drama: Mrs Younger continues to be obsessed with trees and bus queues. This little benefits the quality of work developed in class. Lessons are constantly interrupted by stray people and indeed one doubts the wisdom of using the main corridor as a drama space.

English: Miss Locksley is a personable and charming young lady with an alluring reading voice and a beguiling manner. We have been particularly impressed with the red jumpsuit and are pleased to see her taking such care over her appearance. Her marking scheme is inconsistent and needs looking into, but otherwise it is hard to fault her. A credit to her profession.

French: This poetic language is ill-suited to ranting and bawling. The sooner Monsieur Apricot appreciates this fact the better.

Geography: Mr Underwood showed great presence of mind in organizing the search party for Kev O'Brien during the Lake District field-trip. Nevertheless, the subsequent discovery that Kev was laid up at home with laryngitis and had actually missed the trip in the first place did little to enhance Mr Underwood's reputation with the mountain rescue team. This unfortunate incident has noticeably dented his confidence during the rest of the year. He has our commiserations.

History: Mrs Treadwell's eyesight remains her shortcoming. Unfortunately she misses much off what is going on in class (Dirty Davidson gets away with murder). Her frequent absences and recent hospitalization have further hampered progress. Now may well be the time to start thinking of future plans, e.g. a quiet rest-home in the country.

Mathematics: Mr McIntyre displays an excellent understanding of this subject and obviously fully deserved the double first at Oxford that he so frequently refers to. Perhaps in the coming year he might consider imparting some of his knowledge to his class in language that is more easily understandable.

Physical Education: The school sports day was rained off for the second year in a row. Mr Jennings is believed to have issued thirty-seven detentions in the second half of the summer term. Is this a record, or merely a coincidence?

The Headteacher: D.T. has taught no classes of any description during the past year and is seldom if ever seen around the school. Therefore it is impossible to assess his progress or evaluate what his contribution might be in school life.

Final Comment: This year has been much as other years. Behaviour has been generally good, but we are still concerned about smoking in the stockroom, particularly during lesson periods. Several of the staff have yet to appreciate the school's excellent acoustics. It really is not necessary to bellow at the top of your voice when addressing a child standing right beside you. Overall, fair progress has been made, the staff have worked steadily and shown reasonable ability. There is of course room for improvement. Nobody's perfect.

Signed,
The Pupils

---

1 Discuss the following:
(a) Do you think teaching is a difficult job?
(b) Are reports useful? To whom are they most useful: parents, teachers, pupils or employers?

(c) If you had the choice, what changes would you make in the way reports are presented or used in your own school?

2 List your least favourite subjects and write reports about yourself written from the point of view of that teacher.

3 Write out a list of the subjects you take in school now. Would you like the list to be longer and include other subjects, or be shorter?

4 Act out a scene where a parent or teacher is reading a very critical report with the appropriate pupil. How can the teacher or parent help? What is their best approach? What is the attitude of the pupil?

5 Either as a class or in small groups create through role-play a school of the future. Consider various key moments in the life of the school, e.g. will there be reports? If not, what will replace them or make them irrelevant?

3 PROBLEMS

Bernie's Top Ten

> *For Bernie life is full of frightening experiences, so he tries to decide how best to cope with the problem of perpetually feeling scared.*

There's no point beating about the bush – life frightens me. I don't just mean I'm scared of spiders or stuff like that. After all, nobody likes spiders do they? There's nothing wrong with hating spiders. But the sad awful truth is that I am a complete hundred-per-cent-proof coward. When I die my tombstone will read: 'Here lies Bernie Watts. Please don't tread on the daisies.'

Being scared all the time, you have to be philosophical. It's not so much a problem, more a way of life. Being scared, you realize early on that you'll never climb Everest or stick your head in a lion's mouth or go ten rounds with Mike Tyson. You'll never be an astronaut or join the SAS. Being scared limits your possibilities.

So recently, my mum said what I ought to do is rationalize my anxieties. 'Bernie,' she said, 'rationalize. Once you know what it is you're scared of you can start to do something about it.' That's when I made my list. My top ten. The ten things I'm most scared of. Of course I had to leave a lot of things out, but this is what I finally came up with:

Bernie's Top Ten
1   Dentists
2   Rats, mice, cats, dogs and hamsters
3   All other animals
4   Going to bed with the window open
5   Doing the assault course in gym
6   Going into crowded rooms
7   Kicking my football into Mr Turner's garden
8   Asking Mr Turner for my ball back
9   Being sent down the shops by my mum without a list to remind me what to get
10 All forms of physical pain

Plus I don't much like heights. Or cupboards. Or water or standing on buses or cleaning out the rabbit hutch. Or getting my school report, or kissing my grandmother, or answering the telephone, or having to read out loud in French, or crossing a busy street, or flying in an aeroplane (not that I ever have), or walking down dark alleyways, or falling in love, or getting told off by my mum, or getting told off by my dad, or getting told off by my teachers, or going to the school disco, or being told to keep a secret, or cold rice pudding. Then of course there's all the other things I'm scared of that I don't have time to mention, but more or less those are the main things. Oh yes, and I'm not over keen on roller-coasters.

It's quite a frightening list when you think about it. But, like my mum says, I have to be rational. What can I do about all these fears and anxieties? Now it seems to me I've got three alternatives.

Firstly, I could stop getting up in the morning. Instead of leaping out of bed like a cat jumping out of a bath and panicking about whether I'll miss the bus which will make me late for morning assembly which will get me into everyone's bad books before the day's even begun – instead of going through all that rigmarole, I could just turn off the alarm, turn over and go back to sleep. I mean, why get up? Why ever get up? Why not spend one's whole life wrapped up snugly under the bedclothes? Life doesn't seem so threatening under the bedclothes.

Or secondly, I could get up but try to avoid all the things that I know I'm scared of. I could stop going to the dentist which would mean no more waiting around for hours reading old copies of *National Geographical* and imagining what I'd look like with no teeth. I could pretend I've got laryngitis whenever Monsieur Apricot asks me to read aloud in French, or feign an acute attack of gastric flu every time my mum dishes up cold tinned rice for pudding. I mean, it wouldn't be easy, spending my whole life trying to avoid things. But the way I see it – if you're determined enough you can avoid anything.

Or then there's the third alternative. The psychological approach. Every time I'm faced with one of my fears or anxieties I could tell myself over and over that there's nothing to be worried about. I could try to face up to things. For example, when I see next door's Jack Russell standing in our garden cultivating the roses, instead of bolting the back door and watching it from the kitchen window, willing it to crawl back through the hole in the hedge to where it rightfully belongs, I could go out and throw it a stick or pat it on the head. After all, I once heard Mr Turner tell my dad that it didn't bite everyone. Instead of hiding behind Pincher Perkins next time Mr Jennings wants a volunteer to walk across the high beam in gym, I could put up my hand and give it a go. I'd still be scarred as hell but at least it'd be a challenge. I mean, it's not that dangerous. Dirty Davidson fell off the high beam last Christmas and he only had the plaster on till Easter. Perhaps, maybe, who knows, if I tried a few things they wouldn't be as bad as they seem.

Right then, being rational, all I have to do is to decide which choice to make. Three alternatives: stay in bed; get up but try to avoid life's little unpleasantries; or psyche myself up and face the challenge. A choice – any one from three.

Trouble is, I don't much like decisions. They always seem a bit too final. If you make a decision it could change your whole life. In fact, decisions are just about more frightening than anything else. So how do I decide if I'm going to make a decision? You can appreciate my dilemma.

You know, sometimes I reckon life's not as simple as it ought to be.

---

1 Discuss the following:
  (a) Do you feel that it is possible to 'rationalize' fears and phobias?
  (b) Why do you feel Bernie gets worried about such seemingly ordinary events such as answering the telephone or having to keep a secret? Is he simply a coward, or is there more to it than that?
  (c) How would you define the word 'bravery'?

2 Compile your own Top Ten of fears and anxieties. Compare this list with others in the group, then collate the results of the individual lists to come up with a Group Top Ten. What is the most common worry? Do your results include any of Bernie's top ten fears?

3 In small groups, act out a 'disaster' scene (e.g. stuck in a lift in a burning building, adrift at sea, on a hijacked aeroplane). How do different characters respond to the situation? Perhaps the scene could have a surprise ending – pick out the character you feel is least likely to be able to cope, and show how s/he finally becomes the hero or heroine of the day.

4 In pairs, improvise a scene between a psychiatrist and his/her patient. The patient tells of all the things that scare him/her (they can be as ridiculous as you like) and the psychiatrist must provide a convincing explanation for this fear and a means of overcoming it.

Brief-Case Boy

Bullying is a common problem in many schools. If you have been on the receiving end it can be very painful and worrying. It can also have disturbing consequences.

He pressed himself hard against the wall and prayed they wouldn't notice him. He willed himself to become invisible, his grey anorak merging into the grey stone. No one would see him if he didn't speak or move or breathe.

Big Nose and Blondie headed the mob of fifth-formers. He didn't know their real names and anyway he secretly enjoyed insulting them in his mind. He hardly dared breathe as he watched them sauntering towards the bus stop. Towards him. They spoke loudly, swore frequently, shoved each other and spat on the wet road. Perhaps tonight they would be too engrossed with themselves to bother with an insignificant being like him. But they came closer.

Until two weeks ago he had managed to blend in with all the other new pupils waiting to catch the special bus into the city. Apart from general insults flung at the heads of first-formers no one was picked out for special attention. Then he'd made his first mistake. It was a fatal error. He'd stared at one of them for too long. In fact he hadn't really been looking at anyone in particular, just thinking about his tea and how quickly he could do his homework and watch television.

'What you staring at?'

'Sorry.'

'You soon will be!' The boy who had spoken turned to his mate and pointed at his new victim. The silence was tense, menacing.

'Look, he's carrying a brief-case. Ah! Isn't that nice? A present from mummy was it? Let's have a look.'

The brief-case was snatched from his grasp. It had been a present from his mother right enough, a special gift the day before he started school. 'Now that you're going to secondary school I thought you might need this for your books,' she'd said. 'Take good care of it.' He had been proud and delighted. Now, as he watched the black plastic case being thrown through the air as the fifth-formers hurled it from one to the other he was terrified.

'Oops, missed!' said Blondie, as the case landed scratched and battered at his feet. It burst open and books fell out on to the pavement. The young boy tried to be brave about the situation but it was no good.

'Issum's crying?' one of the fifth-formers asked mockingly.

'Mummy'll kiss him better,' another said, laughing.

Through his tears the boy could see ink running from his case and brown stains appearing on the book covers as size nine boots trampled them into the dirt. His mind was a whirl of angry sobs, the laughter of the youths and a sense of dizziness. He felt confused and powerless.

The next day he carried his books, or the remains of them, in an anonymous plastic bag, but the youths had acquired a taste for inflicting pain and this time they took his bus money. They threw the coins with whoops of laughter into one of the gardens next to the bus stop before they ran off. He had to crawl on his hands and knees amongst the garden plants in a vain attempt to recover them. He did not find his money but was greeted instead by shouts from the owner of the house: 'Get out! I'll report you to your school.'

That evening he walked home and refused to tell his mother why he was late.

That night he wet the bed.

---

1 Discuss what the boy with the brief-case could have done to prevent the bullying. Should he have tried to stand up to the bullies? How else might he have coped with the situation?

2 Divide into two groups: one group are the 'bullies', the second group are the 'bullied'. The bullies issue a series of tasks for the second group to perform. Gradually the second group start to rebel. Improvise what happens next. Then swap roles and see what happens this time. Afterwards discuss at which point members of each group started to rebel and why. How did each group feel when they were playing the 'bullies' and how did they feel when they were being bullied?

The Party

What makes people deliberately set out to vandalize? This story describes the effect of one such act.

It hadn't happened before. Nobody quite knew who had the idea first. But however it first arose it was decided to have a party for the old folks. After all, Christmas isn't anything unless you do something for other people. The sixth-formers were often criticized for being selfish, particularly by the teachers, and here was a chance to prove themselves. They'd had a disco back in November and the £100 it had raised, including the giant raffle, would easily pay for the party.

A committee was formed and the organization began. There was the food to think of: should they all bring things in from home or buy the food from the shops? Then there was the entertainment – old-time songs, a few sketches, someone dressed up as Father Christmas. How would they invite the old folks – by letter perhaps? They enjoyed the planning, and working towards a positive end-product brought the whole sixth form together as a unit. They had done it by themselves, without any help from teachers.

At last the day of the party came. By half past four the room looked very impressive. There were bunches of holly, streamers, balloons. The tables, complete with fancy table coverings and crackers were set in readiness for the guests. The entertainment had been practised for weeks.

The old folks were due to arrive at six o'clock and everybody left to get changed in time to greet the guests. Silence descended in the room, an eerie silence.

Gary had not meant to break into the school at first. With a few of his mates he went to the boiler house, had a few fags and told a few jokes. But it was cold out there and coming on to rain. If they could get into the school it would be warm and dry. The place was deserted and surely at least one window would be open. They wandered around: first the science block – nothing doing; next the gym – not even so much as a broken window.

Then they saw it. It was too good to be true. The door was open. They just walked in. They said nothing for the first few seconds, then it hit them.

'Just look at that!'

'Pretty!'

'All set for a party.'

'Nobody ever gave us a party when we came to this dump.'

'I think we'll have a party of our own, shall we?'

A hand reached for the table cloth and with a violent pull it and all that was on it went hurtling to the ground. Glasses were smashed, flowers trampled underfoot, chairs were broken, tables upturned. Then they set upon the food. Fights with jellies were really a laugh. The trouble was it didn't last long enough. But they'd had their fun.

---

1 Imagine you are the sixth-form students who are organizing the party. Using desks, tables and chairs set up the room you are in as if you were getting ready for the old folks' party. Once you have done this stand back and build a common picture of the scene in your minds – imagining the food, balloons, streamers etc.

Then rearrange the room to represent its vandalized state after the intrusion. Again build a common picture of the scene in your minds – broken chairs, food everywhere, burst balloons etc.

Then come into the room as the sixth formers. What will you say and do? Will the party be able to take place?

2 Divide into three groups: the first group are journalists from a local paper who have been very critical of the school in the past; the second are journalists from a national paper looking for a 'sensational' story; the third are from a national paper trying to give a 'balanced' report. Decide what your approach is to the incident. What will be your headline? You might need to interview members of the sixth form or a teacher at the school. Write your articles and then present them to the rest of the class and discuss the differences between the articles.

There's No Smoke Without . . .

Did you know that a smoker dies every six minutes? Did you know that more girls smoke than boys? If you started to smoke when you were twelve and smoked thirty cigarettes each week until you were sixty how much would you spend? Here is a story about smoking.

The other day we were all sitting in the tiny music room waiting for the teacher to arrive. Mrs Wilson finally appeared and handed out the instruments. Good, I thought, at least it's going to be practical. But no such luck for me. She asked me to go and rinse out the recorders in the toilet sinks. Well, I thought, Lower School toilets aren't far so it shouldn't take too long. But the toilets were locked, so I had to go over to Upper School.

Ten minutes of the lesson had gone already, and I quite like music. When I finally arrived at the toilets in Upper School I tried to balance the recorders in one hand and push the door open with the other. It must have been oiled because I went flying in and landed flat on my face, recorders rolling in every direction.

I could hardly see a thing because the toilets were full of smoke. I hate smoking. Two fifth-form girls were in there, each with a cigarette in her mouth. I didn't know them but I'd seen them around. I got up and scrambled for the recorders. One of the girls kicked a recorder under a toilet door. They both laughed as I went to collect it. I could feel myself blush with embarrassment. Just keep cool, I said to myself. Act as though nothing has happened. I rinsed out the recorders and headed for the door, only to find it blocked by one of the girls.

'And where do you think you're going? she growled.

'Back to Mrs Wilson's class,' I whispered, trying to squeeze out of the door. But I felt a hand grab me.

'You're not.'

I could smell the smoke on her breath and I faked a cough.

'She's not used to smoke,' her friend taunted.

'Perhaps we'd better let her get used to it.'

'If you want no trouble you better just smoke this.'

'Please don't waste your cigarettes on me,' I pleaded.

'It's no waste.'

A cigarette was pushed into my lips.

'You just take a drag.'

I tried to force it out between my lips but the grip tightened around my arm.

'If you want to get out of this without being hurt, just take a drag.'

I blew out as hard as I could but I knew I was beaten. The second girl grabbed hold of my hair. I could feel the pull on my scalp.

'Smoke it.'

I took a breath in. I felt dizzy. I was going to be sick any minute. The grip relaxed and the second girl let go of my hair.

'What a good little girl. Now run off back to class and if you open your mouth about this – well . . . look out for trouble.'

All that was several weeks ago and I haven't said a word to anyone. I haven't seen those two again but sooner or later . . . well, you know. As for smoking, how can anyone do it? As far as I'm concerned that was my first and last cigarette.

I've been thinking about those two girls. Much as I hated them at the time of that incident, I just can't get the thought of them out of my mind. If they smoke a packet of cigarettes every day, they will have spent over £10,000 between them in the next ten years. Just think what you could do with £10,000! Though, what with the health risks, they might not live that long. Smoking – it's a mug's game.

---

1 Working in small groups, make a still picture or tableau of some scenes based on:
   (a) a gang with someone trying a cigarette for the first time
   (b) the secret gang of smokers behind the bike shed at school
   (c) an operation – a surgeon removing a cancerous growth caused by smoking.

2 Using the same groups, make up an advertisement with a suitable slogan or jingle to show the dangers of smoking.

3 Discuss how you can persuade someone who smokes to give up.

Telly Addict

Have you ever counted the number of hours of television you watch in a week? It has been said that if children watch too much television it can have a harmful effect upon their lives. In this story Graham has become a television addict.

Graham couldn't wait to get home. The last lesson of the day always dragged so much. He looked at his watch. It couldn't be right! Half an hour to go. It must be later. He looked again: three-fifteen. Another half-hour of the teacher droning on and four pages to copy up. How he hated school.

At last he was on the bus going home. Even that seemed to be taking hours. The other children laughed and joked, some sang songs, but he just stared out of the window.

'Graham, are you going to Clare's party tonight?'

'No, don't think so.'

'Go on, it'll be a laugh. She wanted you to go you know.'

'I'm not bothered.'

'Please yourself then.'

He was left alone to stare out of the bus window and watch impatiently the trees and fields pass by. When he arrived home he threw his bag on the floor and his coat on the back of the chair.

'Hello Graham, had a good day at school?' his mother asked.

He grunted an inaudible reply and headed for his bedroom. He didn't notice the dirty cups and plates, one with mould growing out of it, nor the jumbled heap of clothes on the floor. All he could see was the shining glass screen of the television. He pressed the switch. If only he wasn't too late.

Colourful cartoon shapes filled the screen. It had just started. It was his favourite cartoon programme and he settled down to watch it. Everything else faded from his mind – teachers, school, his mother – nothing mattered except the cartoon fantasy.

Two hours later and he had barely moved. Programmes had come and gone but still he watched. His mother brought him a meal. He swallowed mouthfuls still with his eyes on the screen, completely unaware of what he was eating. It might as well have been soil or cardboard.

The late-night movie was special tonight. It was all about a strange creature appearing and disappearing out of the fog and mist. His heart missed a beat as he watched it. He clenched his fists. He could feel himself go hot and cold.

The next day was much the same as the previous one. Panic on the bus to copy up homework missed from the previous day, a blank from nine till four, and then life began when he switched on the television set.

The following day the school closed for an occasional day's holiday. His mother had to go to work and left Graham to organize things at home. You can guess what happened. There were no pots washed, no food cooked and there was a mess everywhere.

'Graham, I don't know what is going to become of you.'

'Sorry, Mum.'

'It's no good being sorry. I've been out at work all day and all you've done is watch television. We can't carry on like this, can we?'

Graham knew in his heart that his mother was right, the trouble was, how could he change?

1 Arrange yourselves in pairs. One of you knows nothing about television, for example you are from another planet or a character from the past. The other person describes all he or she can about television – how it works, the programmes etc. After you have done this, discuss with the rest of the class the implications of the game.

2 Organize a debate on 'We would all be far better off if television had not been invented.'

3 Discuss what advice you would give to Graham and his mother about his addiction.

One Good Turn

> *Life revolves around the favours we do for each other. It is part of human nature to help those in need, whether it be the next-door neighbour or starving millions in Africa. But doing the 'right thing' won't always bring gratitude.*

The man's name was Mr Hardcastle and he lived at 29 Freeman Avenue. Joe recognized the name of the street. It was across town on a large residential estate. The journey would mean either two changes of bus or a long walk. Was it really worth the effort?

Joe looked once more through the wallet. Apart from Mr Hardcastle's driving licence, it contained a photograph of Mrs Hardcastle (or someone who might easily be Mrs Hardcastle, if Mr Hardcastle was indeed married), several credit cards and a dental appointment card. But what gave the wallet its weight and bulk was the money: three £10 notes and six, no seven, fivers. This man must have been either very careless or just plain stupid to have lost something like that.

'Sixty-five quid!' Joe muttered to himself. The wallet in his hand was worth sixty-five pounds! It was a daunting, even frightening thought. For a moment Joe tried to think of all the things he could buy for sixty-five pounds. Then he pushed the dreams aside. If I return the wallet I'm bound to get a good reward, thought Joe. He could just picture Mr Hardcastle's face beaming with gratitude at the return of the lost wallet. There could be a tenner or more in a good deed like that. Joe put the wallet into his pocket and set off on the long journey to Freeman Avenue.

It was not a very large house; a semi, with a neat little lawn in the front, just like all the other houses on the estate. A blue Metro was parked in the drive and Joe could hear people moving around inside even as he approached the front door. The housing estate might be private, but the houses certainly weren't with their wide plate windows and thin walls. Joe stood at the door and listened to the voices. There were two people talking heatedly, having a big argument by the sound of things. Joe felt a strange sense of power. In a minute he would ring the doorbell and be able to put an end to their feuding. The missing wallet had returned.

He knocked. The door was opened by a young woman in an old dressing-gown. She looked at Joe in an angry, impatient manner.

'Yes, what is it?' she demanded.

'Um, is Mr Hardcastle at home please?' Joe asked.

The woman went back into the house, leaving Joe stranded on the doorstep. 'Sid, it's for you. Some kid,' he heard her say.

Mr Hardcastle came to the door. He was wearing a business suit and looked fairly affable.

'And what can I do for you, son?' he asked.

Joe took the wallet from his pocket and handed it to Mr Hardcastle. 'I found this outside the post office. I think it's yours.'

'What?' Mr Hardcastle looked surprised. He put his hand into the back pocket of his trousers. 'My word, you're right. It is mine.'

'You must have dropped it, Sir,' Joe said.

'Yes indeed.' The man opened the wallet and checked the contents. 'Thank you very much, son. I'd have been in deep trouble if you hadn't found this. There's quite a bit of money in here.'

'Yes, Sir, I know.'

Mr Hardcastle smiled and placed the wallet in his pocket. Joe stood and watched him, uncertain of what to do or say. Was that it? Surely Mr

Hardcastle wasn't going to let him go without showing his appreciation in some way?

'Yes, well, thanks again,' the man said.

'No trouble,' replied Joe, rooted to the spot.

Mr Hardcastle smiled broadly and put his hand in his jacket pocket. Out came a fifty-pence piece which he offered to Joe. 'Here you are son – a token of my appreciation.'

'Eh?' Joe looked at the coin with disgust.

'No, please take it,' said the man , 'it's the least you deserve.'

Mr Hardcastle patted the boy on the shoulder and then closed the front door, leaving Joe alone in the drive with the measly fifty-pence coin in his hand. 'Some gratitude!' Joe mumbled as he turned away from the house. 'Fifty pence! What a waste of time and effort!'

Joe stopped at the end of the drive and looked back at the house. He could just picture Mr Hardcastle inside, laughing his head off as he gleefully counted out his newly found banknotes. He listened, but all he could hear was the sound of crashing objects and two angry voices, one male one female, shouting loudly at each other. Joe shrugged his shoulders and began his long walk home. Some people are so selfish, he thought to himself.

---

1 Discuss the following:

(a) Do you feel Joe is hard done by in receiving only a fifty-pence reward? Is his behaviour any less 'selfish' than Mr Hardcastle's?

(b) What do you think it is that motivates people to do good deeds?

(c) Have you ever found something that belonged to somebody else? If so, can you remember what you did about it?

(d) How far do you believe in the sentiment: 'Finders keepers'?

2 Get three people to improvise the following situation: A and B are sitting in the park. They both see a £10 note lying by the bench and A claims it. There is a difference of opinion – A intends to keep the money; B thinks it should be handed in to the police. A and B try and convince each other of their case. When a decision has been reached, C enters looking for the lost £10 note. What happens next? Do A and B hand over the money? Is C grateful?

3 In three groups act out one of the following:

(a) 'Its better to give than to receive.'

(b) 'Charity begins at home.'

(c) 'God helps those who help themselves.'

Lies

Have you ever told a lie? Someone once said that the world couldn't exist unless people did! When is a lie just a harmless exaggeration of the truth and when is it dishonest? Kevin is thirteen and is thinking about lies.

The other day my mate told me about a dog that scored a goal in a football match. Sounds ridiculous doesn't it? He reckons that it was in a cup match and the teams were level when this dog called Lucky runs on to the pitch. There's confusion in the penalty area, the referee is unsighted, the dog heads the ball, the ball crosses the line – goal! Players protest, players are sent off, punch up! But the goal stands.

Now I trust my mate, he doesn't usually lie about things but, well, I ask you! A goal scored by a dog? Crazy! He must have seen too much telly or read too many books.

People tell you lies to impress you, don't they? You know the type of thing: Dad owns his own company, drives a Rolls Royce; Mum's a model with a fashion magazine – all that load of old rubbish. We had a new lad in our class last term who started telling stories. After a while everyone knew it was lies because the stories were so crazy. Next thing he's got no friends, everyone just ignores him. The question is, why did he start to tell those lies in the first place? It seemed that once he'd started he just couldn't stop.

My dad tells stories of his youth – that's when he's in a good mood or he's got the time – and when he's telling them, well, I just wonder. Take the one he told a couple of weeks ago. He was sixteen at the time and went pot-holing with the youth club. Most of the group hadn't been before and were very nervous about the prospect of small spaces miles underground. So the youth-club leader took them to the pub the night before to calm their nerves and help them relax. He arranged a special room for the group to be in by themselves and everyone promised to have soft drinks and no alcohol. Trouble was that not everyone kept their promise.

The leader explained basic safety-rules when pot-holing and the need to act with caution. He left the room to go to the toilet for a few minutes. When he came back he was amazed at what he found. Dad was stuck under a coffee table. He had crawled under the legs of the table, which was attached to the floor, imagining he was in a small space underground, and he was well and truly stuck. The youth-club leader told him to come out and not to be so silly, but Dad was stuck. Twenty minutes later, and the group were still dismantling the coffee table, trying to release a panic-stricken dad.

He never did go underground – good job I say. But the question is, is it the truth? I don't mean that Dad has deliberately lied by making the whole thing up – after all, I know that he is accident-prone. But perhaps he has let his imagination run away with him. He so enjoyed telling the funny story that I think he was exaggerating certain parts of it. Could he really have been stuck under that table for twenty minutes? The incident happened some years ago and maybe Dad's memory isn't a hundred-per-cent accurate. If I could ask the other youth-club members what actually happened, they would probably all give different versions. Besides, I've heard Dad tell other stories about his youth and every time he tells one particular story the details change.

Makes you wonder if there is such a thing as truth doesn't it? Like in court, when a policeman and suspect give their account of something, they might be talking about two completely different events.

1 Try this game: Chinese Whispers. Stand the class in a long line. The teacher whispers a message to the first person, who then whispers it to the next person, and so on to the end of the line. What is the message at the end of the line? Has the game any link with the theme of the story?

2 Act out a scene where gossip distorts the truth. The consequences may be humorous or serious.

3 Discuss if there are times when it might be better to tell a lie than the truth. Or should one always tell the truth, even if it hurts someone?

It Won't Affect Me

One of the most serious problems affecting young people today is drug addiction. This story describes what happened to one boy. It is told by his mother.

I don't know why or how it happened. I just don't understand. I am talking about my son, Paul, who is sixteen. He's never been a problem child and I don't think we as his parents neglected him. We've always got on so well. He's never been in trouble with the police before, and now this terrible thing has happened.

Paul seemed happy. He had his own computer and television in his bedroom and even a pool table in the spare room. I went out to work so we could have those few extras. He and his dad never had any big arguments, only what most teenagers have with their parents. The police asked if being the only child in the family had made him lonely but he never seemed unhappy. I thought a boy in his teens would be easier to look after than a girl. No problems with pregnancy or things like that.

I try to tell myself that it has been one big mistake and that soon I'll wake up from this nightmare. The police say that Paul started sniffing glue some months ago. 'Did you notice anything strange about your son during the last few months?' they asked. Well, he was quieter than usual, I will admit that. I thought it was the worry of his exams that are coming up soon. We had plans for him to stay on in the sixth form. But now, after this, who can tell?

Then it seems that Paul and his friend Dan went from glue to drugs. Dan has been a good friend for some time and has regularly come round to our house. I know his mother quite well. They took the drugs in the garage round at Dan's house. Quite what kind of drugs they were still isn't clear, not that it really matters. Then, when they were high on drugs they had some kind of argument and Paul tipped petrol over Dan and set fire to him. He is in intensive care now in hospital and I have been brought to the police station where the police are holding Paul. They haven't let me see him yet and they say he is still being interviewed.

What shall I say to him? What kind of mother am I who brings up a boy who does that to somebody? What kind of monster would tip petrol over his best friend and set fire to him?

They say that it is so easy to buy drugs these days and that in pubs and clubs they are part of the everyday scene. If that is so, perhaps those who sell them should visit the hospital right now to see poor Dan or go to the police station to see Paul.

---

1 Discuss the following:
   (a) Why do you think Paul took drugs? Extend the discussion to talk about why you think young people take drugs.
   (b) Paul's mother doesn't know what to say to her son. What advice would you give her? She says: 'We've always got on so well.' Do you think this is true?

2 In small groups act out key moments in Paul's life:
   (a) A family scene just before he first tries drugs.
   (b) His first experiment with drugs – where is he? Who is he with?
   (c) The conversation with his mother at the police station.
   (d) Sometime in the future.

Being Different

> *Do you think that men and women are equal? Do you think that society treats them as equals? Are there jobs that only women should do? This story is concerned with the equality of the sexes and is told by Alison.*

You could say that our family is different. For a start, Dad stays at home whilst Mum goes out to work. It started when my brother Mick and I were born. We're twins and Mum said that she didn't think that she could cope with two babies, two mouths to feed, two nappies to change. Dad said he thought he could, so he gave up his job and Mum went back to work. It just so happened that Dad hated his nine-to-five routine and Mum had a good job in a bank. I admire them for doing it, but they took some stick from their friends, parents and neighbours.

It seemed so natural to Mick and me as we grew up that we didn't give it a second thought. That is until we started school. Then it was our turn to take some stick: What's that – your dad makes your clothes? Your dad will make the costumes for the school play? Why not your mum? We learned to cope with it most of the time but some comments – Why have you got such a weird family? – really hurt.

It didn't help when Mick and I started to adopt our own different lifestyles. As it happens, I'm good at mechanical things – putting on a new tap washer, changing a fuse, adjusting the vacuum cleaner. Don't laugh, I really enjoy these things, whereas Mick loves horse riding and cooking.

Some people think that we're just freaks and cross the street to avoid us. Our next-door neighbours put their house up for sale and Dad says it was because of us. I can't really believe that. We're not anti-social or anything. Perhaps it's just that people expect us to conform to their stereotype: girls wear pink, boys wear blue. Even at infant school I was given dolls to play with and Mick was given soldiers. Why should it be like that? Why do people feel threatened by something that doesn't conform to their own values? Mick's got a girlfriend and I think she understands. With me it's more difficult. My last boyfriend and I finished when I fixed his car while all he could do was curse at it. Only last month we had a real problem. The problem was called Grandad. He's always lived alone, but he's eighty now and his large house is getting too much for him. He has trouble getting his breath and can't climb stairs. Dad's offered to let him stay with us this winter so we can keep an eye on him. The trouble is that Grandad never understood our way of life. I can hear him now: 'A grown man changing nappies? That's not right. That's woman's work. Why don't you get a proper job?' He and Mum never got on. 'Never let a woman rule your life' is one of his favourite sayings which we'll hear ad nauseam.

But that problem paled into insignificance compared with the latest one our lifestyle caused. Mick won a cookery competition. Why's that a problem? I can hear you thinking. After all most boys do cooking in schools these days. The trouble was caused by the account of the competition in the local newspaper. Mick was the only male contestant in the regional final. The headline was: 'Michael puts the Ladies to shame'. There was a picture of him with his prize cake surrounded by all the girls. Mum and Dad were so proud of him, little did they know the unhappiness the newspaper account caused.

Mick went to the school the next day and a gang from his class were waiting for him. They taunted him about the competition and when Mick tried to ignore them they attacked him. He ran home and when I saw the state he was in I wanted to know what had happened. After some time he reluctantly told me the story but pleaded with me not to tell anyone. He didn't want Mum or Dad to know or any of the teachers in case it caused more trouble and now I don't know what I should do. It's all caused by us being that little bit different, but I don't see why we should change, do you?

---

1 Alison says she doesn't know what to do. Working in small groups talk over the situation of the family and agree about what advice you would offer her and the rest of the family. Then ask four members of the class to take the various roles of the family. Once this has been decided, report back your advice to them. How do they feel about the advice? Would they like to ask any questions? As a conclusion to this, discuss what the future might hold for the family if they act upon the advice given.

2 Look through magazines, videos, books etc. Do you see any evidence of sexual stereotyping in the depiction of men or women? If you do, consider what influence this might have upon the way we view our roles.

3 Act out a scene where a group discriminates on the basis of gender, e.g. an interview for a job, joining a club or team, a scene in school. Then discuss the scene. Why does discrimination take place?

Appendix

Title	Issues
Beep Click	Computers; generation gap
Being Different	Role reversal; victimization; defensive attitudes
Bernie in Love	First love; romantic delusion
Bernie's Big Race	Competition; personal achievement; mistakes
Bernie's Family	Family relationships; selfishness; complaining
Bernie's Report	School reports; making judgements; purpose of criticism
Bernie's Top Ten	Fears and phobias; rationalizing problems
Brief-Case Boy	Bullying; power; self-image
Dog's Life, A	Pets; sense of purpose
Empty House, The	Running away; coping with grief
Enough is Enough	Rumours; first impressions; changing attitudes
First Meeting	Love and its development
Great Divide, The	Perseverance; peer-group dynamics
Grey Hair	Ageing; insensitivity; parents as people
Happy Ending	Old age; relationships with older people; helping others
Hollywood Dream, The	Work and people's attitudes to it; dreams and ambitions
Invaders	Horror films; power of the imagination
It Won't Affect Me	Drug addiction; parental responsibility
Leaving Home	Leaving home; independence
Lies	Lies, fibs and telling stories
Mini	Attitudes to possessions
One Good Turn	Charitable acts and motives; gratitude
Owning Up	Betrayal; guilt; self-protection
Party, The	Vandalism; thoughtlessness; the consequences of actions
Pennine Way, The	Charity; priorities; making sacrifices
Protest, The	Animal rights; matters of principle; personal morality
Sands of Time, The	Power of memories; nostalgia and change; pollution
Snowman	Dangerous play; rashness
Super Gran	Perseverance; achievement; ageism
Telly Addict	TV addiction; escapism, selfishness
There's No Smoke Without ...	Smoking; bullying
Watching	Accidents; death; dares; heroism